AUNT BRANWELL

AND THE

BRONTË LEGACY

AUNT BRANWELL

AND THE

BRONTË LEGACY

Nick Holland

PEN & SWORD
HISTORY

First published in Great Britain in 2018 by
PEN AND SWORD HISTORY
an imprint of
Pen and Sword Books Ltd
47 Church Street
Barnsley
South Yorkshire S70 2AS

ISBN 978 1 52672 223 2

Printed and bound in the UK
by T J International, Padstow, Cornwall, PL28 8RW

Typeset in Times New Roman 11/13.5 by
Aura Technology and Software Services, India

Pen & Sword Books Ltd incorporates the imprints of Pen & Sword
Archaeology, Atlas, Aviation, Battleground, Discovery,
Family History, History, Maritime, Military, Naval, Politics, Railways,
Select, Social History, Transport, True Crime, Claymore Press,
Frontline Books, Leo Cooper, Praetorian Press, Remember When,
Seaforth Publishing and Wharncliffe.

For a complete list of Pen and Sword titles please contact
Pen and Sword Books Limited
47 Church Street, Barnsley, South Yorkshire, S70 2AS, England
E-mail: enquiries@pen-and-sword.co.uk
Website: www.pen-and-sword.co.uk

Contents

Acknowledgements

There are many people I need to thank for their invaluable support and encouragement during the writing and publishing of this book, not least my family and friends. I also wish to thank the readers of my blog, www.annebronte.org, and of my previous books for their continued support and kind comments.

I have found Pen and Sword Books a pleasure to work with, so great thanks go to all the team there in my home town of Barnsley, and I look forward to working with you all again. Thank you for helping to bring the story of Elizabeth Branwell to life.

Thanks, as always, to everyone at the Brontë Parsonage Museum, from Ann Dinsdale and Sarah Laycock who do such important work expanding and managing the collection, to Danielle Cadamarteri and her team at the museum shop, and indeed to all the amazing volunteers who give up their time because of their love of the Brontës.

Thank you to Victoria Reece-Romain and the team behind the Q Fund, who in the name of Cornish writer Sir Arthur Quiller-Couch have helped me and many others write books about the wonderful county of Cornwall, and the people from it. Thanks also to Rachel Viney and all at the Penzance Literary Festival, and to Melissa Hardie-Budden and the Hypatia Trust, experts on the Branwell and Carne families.

Thank you to Janet Brown for the use of her photograph of the Brontë Parsonage, and to the National Portrait Gallery, and also to Sarah Mason Walden of Nashville, Tennessee, a Brontë expert, enthusiast and collector. Thank you also to expert handwriting analyst Jean Elliott, genealogist Ian Argall, the British Library, the National Archives and the Brotherton Library.

Finally, thank you for reading my book. I hope you enjoy it.

Preface

Three sisters, born in a crowded, somewhat dilapidated, mid-terraced building in Thornton between 1816 and 1820, went on to become the most famous writing family in the world. They were Charlotte, Emily and Anne Brontë, and would become synonymous with the village their father moved to just four months after the birth of Anne, his sixth and final child; Haworth.

As a Yorkshireman myself, I'm very proud to be from the same county that produced, against all odds, such genius. The creators of *Jane Eyre*, *Wuthering Heights*, and *The Tenant of Wildfell Hall*, among other works, are to my mind the queens of Yorkshire – and yet their roots and influences lay far away from the Pennine moorlands they called home.

Many people know that their father, Patrick Brontë, was an Anglican priest originally from County Down in what is now Northern Ireland, and indeed that his name wasn't Brontë at all originally, as he changed it from the all too obviously Irish Brunty or Prunty. Many people also know of the sad early demise of the Brontës' mother, Maria, who died when her youngest child Anne was just one year old. Originally from Penzance, Cornwall, her tragic death in 1821 denied the young Brontës a mother, and explains why they were influenced by Ireland but not Cornwall. This is well known, but like many well-known things, it is in fact wrong.

Maria Bronte's death was indeed a terrible tragedy for her husband and children, but they were not denied a mother figure as they grew up as that role was taken on admirably and courageously by her eldest sister, Elizabeth Branwell. Originally arriving in Haworth in the summer of 1821 to nurse her sick sister, Elizabeth remained to help raise her nephew and nieces in the way that she felt their mother would have wanted.

This action is a true measure of the woman who gave up the pleasant life she had known in the warmth of south-west England for a new home 400 miles away – a home in a harsh environment and in a village where sickness and death was endemic, where the accents and customs were foreign to her, and where the cold, wuthering winds seemed to blow ceaselessly.

It was a substantial sacrifice, and, once made, it became a permanent one – she remained in Haworth for more than two decades until her death, never seeing the familiar Cornish seascapes again.

The writing of the Brontë sisters has been a part of my life since I first picked up *Wuthering Heights* as an 18-year-old student, and like many other people across the world I've found their life stories just as fascinating as the masterpieces of fiction they crafted. As a Brontë biographer I became particularly interested in the common perception of Elizabeth Branwell, or Aunt Branwell as she became known to her charges. Thanks largely to Elizabeth Gaskell's early, and brilliant, biography of her friend Charlotte Brontë, it is easy to get the impression that Aunt Branwell was stern, resentful, unloving almost. This interpretation, however, is one completely at odds with Branwell Brontë's lament that his aunt was 'the guide and director of all the happy days connected with my childhood.'[1]

My aim in writing this, the first ever biography of Elizabeth Branwell, is to create a more faithful impression of the woman who became such an influence on the Brontë sisters and their brother. She was not only their childhood guide, she it was who shaped their characters and personalities, supported their education, and encouraged their creativity. As we shall see, without one very specific input that she had in their lives, there would have been no Brontë books.

We will also look at the Branwell family of Penzance as a whole, and see how their story often mirrored that of the Brontës of Yorkshire. In examining this less than familiar branch of the family, we'll discover how another Brontë aunt left England to start a new life in a new continent – and how her descendants are now the only surviving members of the Branwell line. Now living in a location far removed from Penzance, and from Haworth, they are the closest living relatives of the Brontë sisters in the world.

Writing this book has not been easy, but it has been hugely rewarding. Elizabeth Branwell left behind no letters or writings of her own, but by looking at pronouncements upon her by the Brontës, including veiled appearances in Brontë novels, and others who knew her well, we can get a fuller picture of this woman who became so central to the lives of Charlotte, Branwell, Emily and Anne. It is time to take a fresh look at Elizabeth Branwell, and acknowledge both her qualities as a woman, and her pivotal role in the Brontë legacy that we all enjoy today. To find the real Aunt Branwell, we must begin our journey by travelling to the Cornish peninsula in the eighteenth century.

Chapter 1

The Region of Enchantment

'The island was fifty miles in circumference and certainly it appeared more like the region of enchantment or a beautiful fiction than sober reality ... from a beautiful grove of winter roses and twining woodbine, towers a magnificent palace of pure white marble whose elegant and finely wrought pillars seem the work of mighty Genii and not of feeble men.'

Charlotte Brontë, *Tales of the Islanders*

The Brontë Parsonage Museum in Haworth is a magical building that continues to attract tourists from across the globe, literary pilgrims who share the dream of getting closer to the everyday lives of the genius siblings Charlotte, Emily and Anne Brontë. Among the treasures on show, the clothing worn by the Brontës is a particular draw to many, and standing in front of the dress that Charlotte Brontë wore to her wedding in 1854, for example, can bring an awed silence to the most vocal visitor.

For me, however, it is a smaller, less obtrusive, item of clothing that holds a particular fascination. With so many treasures in their collection, the staff at the museum rotate their exhibits regularly, but one item often features within a glass-topped cabinet in the room now billed as 'Charlotte's Room'. Easily passed over, they are a pair of pattens that were worn frequently by a woman central to the Brontë story, but about whom most people know very little; Elizabeth Branwell.

Pattens are wood- or metal-soled overshoes that are attached to the everyday footwear. In the first half of the nineteenth century, they were typically added to shoes when walking outdoors to protect the footwear from mud and water and to give added grip. Elizabeth Branwell, however, wore her pattens indoors, as reported to Charlotte Brontë's biographer Elizabeth Gaskell:

'I have heard that Miss Branwell always went about the house in pattens, clicking up and down the stairs, from her dread of catching cold.'[1]

1

This sentence encapsulates what makes these otherwise unassuming items so important to me; they are a perfect embodiment of the sacrifice that Elizabeth Branwell made. We shall read later how and why Elizabeth travelled from Penzance to Haworth in 1821, but we should not underestimate the huge sacrifice she was making. One of the greatest hardships she bore was the vast difference in climate between the invariably temperate Cornwall and the frequently wild Yorkshire, but rather than return to the weather, and the town, she loved, Elizabeth instead wore her pattens inside and out, and did her best to ignore the cold winds stealing underneath the doorways and through the floorboards. There can be little doubt that if she had not chosen to stay, pattens and all, we would not have the remarkable Brontë novels that are so loved today.

There was certainly a great difference in weather and temperature between Haworth and Penzance, and it's easy to think that everything must have seemed alien to Elizabeth Branwell after her arrival at the parsonage building that would become her final home, but in fact she found certain similarities between the two locations, in spite of the 400 miles separating them.

Other than the Brontë Parsonage itself there is one other attraction that visitors to Haworth long to see – the moors. At the summit of the village they stretch away from the parsonage building on three sides, and became known and loved by all the Brontë children. Stern and bleak in winter they are transformed by a crown of purple heather in late summer, and yet whatever the season they were a source of magic and enchantment to the Brontës, and to Emily and Anne in particular.

Walking across the Pennine moors around Haworth can bring a sense of wonderment as we realise that we're walking the paths trodden by the feet of the Brontës two centuries earlier. Some locations are particularly evocative, such as the ramshackle ruin of Top Withens, the location if not the actual building portrayed in *Wuthering Heights*, and the Brontë falls with its nearby rock, the Brontë seat, where the sisters sat and discussed life, nature and their childhood tales.

Another such location is Ponden Kirk, a megalithic tower of gritstone rock that rises as a cliff from the moors around three miles to the west of Haworth Parsonage. This outcrag is an imposing feature in itself but what particularly draws the eye is the tall slender hole in the middle of its lower portion. This opening is just large enough for children or young adults to crawl through. Myths have surrounded this strange natural phenomenon for centuries, but by the time of the Brontës it had become known as the fairy cave. It was commonly known, if maybe only half-believed, that passing through this hole brought good fortune to newly married couples, but that unmarried couples who crawled through together would die within a year if they did not marry each other; if they married someone else they were doomed to commit suicide and their spirit would thereafter haunt the cave forevermore[2].

Ponden Kirk was a feature much loved by Emily Brontë, and the area is recreated under the guise of Penistone Crag in *Wuthering Heights*, in which the fairy cave is referenced on three occasions, including Catherine's death-bed recollection of it to Nelly:

> 'This bed is the fairy cave under Penistone Crag, and you are gathering elf-bolts to hurt our heifers; pretending, while I am near, that they are only locks of wool. That's what you'll come to fifty years hence: I know you are not so now. I'm not wandering, you're mistaken, or I should believe you really *were* that withered hag, and I should think I *was* under Penistone Crag[3].'

Catherine's end is nearly upon her, but doubtless she is thinking of happier times in her childhood; she crawled through the fairy cave entrance with Heathcliff but did not marry him, and now, as the legend prophecies, she has to die. It is clear that Emily was conversant with this folkore, and local mythology runs like a rich vein throughout her novel – half remembrances of stories told to her by the much-loved elderly servant Tabby Aykroyd but also, as we shall see, stories told to her by her Aunt Branwell.

When walking near Ponden Kirk today, particularly in mist or when dark clouds gather overhead, it is easy to picture two girls walking ahead of us, hand in hand as they so frequently were – it is Anne and Emily, walking through the rectangular hole in Penistone Kirk. But wait, the mist clears and we see what appears to be the same moorland landscape and two girls, hand in hand approach a hole in the rock and crawl through it, but now the ancient rock and the hole within it are circular. We are seeing an earlier generation of children – this is Maria and Elizabeth Branwell at the Men-an-Tol, a mysterious stone structure left behind by an unknown civilisation that stands three miles west of Penzance. The stone is said to have healing powers, and so for centuries, children with rickets were passed, unclothed, through it nine times as a cure – nine being the number of magic[4]. Another legend says that if a woman crawls through Men-an-Tol backwards under the light of a full moon she will soon become pregnant.

The moorland landscape stretching around Men-an-Tol and around Ponden Kirk shares the same bleak beauty, belying the hundreds of miles that lie between them. The moors of Haworth must have seemed strangely familiar to Elizabeth Branwell when she first arrived there, and it was some comfort to her to discover that the landscape of this westernmost outpost of Yorkshire had a great deal in common with the landscape she knew so well from West Penwith, the westernmost outpost of Cornwall and of the island of Britain as a whole.

There is one other element that the areas around Haworth and Penzance share; they are both lands filled with ancient legends, lands where the supernatural has coincided alongside the everyday for century after century, lands that are a perfect breeding ground for storytellers. One example, the Cornish piskie, has become an emblem of Elizabeth's home county, much loved by tourists and gift shops, but at the turn of the nineteenth century many people really believed in the existence of these little folk, and attributed to them all manner of ills, from poor crops to sick livestock. It was even said they would sometimes swap a human child for one of their own, leaving behind a changeling who was sure to wreak havoc in the family who raised them.

As the nineteenth century wore on, piskie apparitions became increasingly rare in local folklore as the chronicler Samuel Drew noted in 1824:

> 'The age of piskays, like that of chivalry, is gone. There is, perhaps, at present hardly a house they are reputed to visit. They neither steal children, nor displace domestic articles. Even the fields and lanes which they formerly frequented seem to be nearly forsaken. Their music is rarely heard; and they appear to have forgotten to attend their ancient midnight dance. The diffusion of knowledge, by which the people have been enlightened during the last half century, has considerably reduced the numbers of piskays; and even the few that remain, are evidently preparing to take their departure[5].'

The author of this piece, Samuel Drew, was one of the early-nineteenth century renaissance-men that Cornwall specialised in. Born in St Austell in 1765, he may well have been known to the Branwell family of Penzance, as he was a Methodist theologian and writer of local renown. To Drew, there was no contradiction between a deeply held belief in God and a belief in Cornish legends such as the piskies. These were tales that Elizabeth Branwell grew up with, and she later related them to the Brontë children as they sat by her voluminous skirt, enraptured by her tales of olden days and the old folks on cold Yorkshire evenings.

If the piskies were disappearing, other signs of folk beliefs were still very much in evidence around Penzance. The stones of Men-an-Tol are just one reminder of an ancient civilisation that once called Cornwall its home. Other stones are scattered profusely in wild, remote places, bearing testament to the activity of druids and followers of a forgotten brand of paganism. Religion of one kind or another has always been of huge significance in Cornwall, and we shall see how in Elizabeth Branwell's time, the growth of Methodism had a great impact on her life, and later on the lives of her nieces. It is the land of 100 saints, and a brief glimpse at a map of Cornwall reveals how they remember holy men and women that have been long-forgotten elsewhere. After all, who were Saint Ia (commemorated in St Ives), Saint Austol (after whom St Austell is named), Saint Nunne or Saint Just?

Penzance itself, where Elizabeth Branwell was born and grew up, has the meaning of 'holy headland', and tradition says that it was named in honour of a church dedicated to St Anthony, built in the first millennium and now long since gone. The meaning of the name Penwith, however, shows another side of the history of this part of Cornwall, for it translates as 'headland of slaughter'.

Cornwall's coastline winds along through sheltered coves, large natural ports and rocky outcrops for nearly 300 miles. This has made it a centre of Britain's fishing industry today, in Elizabeth Branwell's time, and for thousands of years before that. The long inviting coastline has also made Cornwall a cultural melting pot from the earliest days, and each visiting civilisation soon settled down and added their own stamp to the region.

The earliest inhabitants of Cornwall were Neolithic people who began to settle there around 6,000 years ago. Two thousand years later, we find evidence of a Bronze Age people, with tools and weapons cast in this metal still being uncovered by archaeologists. These people also left behind many of the burial mounds and stone circles scattered about West Penwith, although these monuments were also added to by the next Cornish settlers – the Celts.

Celtic traces can be found in all the extremities of the British Isles; Cornwall, Wales, Ireland and Scotland. The Celts were, however, a nomadic people whose origins lay in Asia. Pottery and other archaeological finds dating from this time, the first millennium BC, show that the Cornish Celts were already trading with Welsh and Irish merchants, and with those who had sailed from France and Spain.

The Celts also brought their ancient pagan religion, at the head of which were the Druids. Knowledge of their religious beliefs and practices were passed on verbally, and so much of their lore is lost, but we know they were nature-loving Pagans who believed in the dual existence of the visual, every-day, world and a hidden world of the spirits. Could it be from Aunt Branwell's tales of the druids of Cornwall that Emily Brontë began to formulate her own beliefs and ideas? Certainly, Emily did eventually embrace her own form of pagan belief where nature held supremacy over all else, and in her poems, she often talks of a hidden power or spirit that visits her. An example of this can be seen in her visionary poem 'The Philosopher':

> 'I saw a spirit, standing, man,
> Where thou doth stand – an hour ago,
> And round his feet three rivers ran,
> Of equal depth, and equal flow -
> A golden stream – and one like blood;
> And one like sapphire seemed to be;
> But, where they joined their triple flood,
> It tumbled in an inky sea[6].'

One possible reason that the Celtic peoples, and Druidism, have left more of a mark on Cornwall than on other parts of England, is that the region was largely untouched by the Roman conquest of Britain. It was, however, known to the Roman writer and historian Diodorus Siculus who wrote:

> 'The inhabitants of that part of Britain which is called Belerion
> [meaning 'Shining Land', the area we now know as West
> Penwith] are very fond of strangers, and from their intercourse
> with foreign merchants are civilised in their manner of life.'[7]

During Elizabeth's childhood in Penzance, she would have seen constant reminders of ancient times and ancient beliefs, whether walking the lanes where pixies were said to reside, or walking past standing stones, menhirs and dolmens left by the druids and the Bronze Age people that came before them.

Elizabeth was a very devout woman, however, and so she would have found more edification from another site that greeted her eyes every day. Visible from the home she grew up in on Market Street, it is a breath-taking building centred upon an island; the monastery of St Michael's Mount.

St Michael's Mount dominates the bay around Penzance, and although perched upon a tidal island usually cut off by the sea, at low tides it can be walked to from the nearest village of Marazion, five miles to the east of Penzance. Home to a monastery since the eighth century, it is a supremely beautiful building with a fascinating history. Almost since its creation it was a destination for pilgrims from across Europe, but in 1275, the original church was destroyed by an earthquake. An even more lavish priory was built on the same site, but its natural defences meant that it often served a military, as well as religious, purpose.

Throughout the centuries whenever conflicts occurred, St Michael's Mount seemed to find itself involved. During the Wars of the Roses it was kept under siege for half a year by Edward IV, and it was also besieged during the English Civil War a century-and-a-half later. In 1497, it was held by Perkin Warbeck, who claimed he was the rightful king of England, and many Cornish people then joined him on his ill-fated march to London.

By Elizabeth Branwell's time the island also had a thriving community living at the foot of the old monastery, and in the early decades of the nineteenth century it had three schools, an equal number of public houses and its own Methodist chapel. Elizabeth must surely have visited St Michael's Mount on many occasions, and would have talked of it to the Brontë children, wistfully describing not only its history, full of battles and adventures, but also its stunning appearance at sunset when it looks almost like marble, surrounded by a fiery glow. It was these tales, at least in part, that led to the Brontës' youthful love of islands, and it is St Michael's Mount, forever imprinted on the memory of the Yorkshire-exiled Elizabeth, that is recreated as the magical palace in her niece Charlotte's youthful work *Tales Of The Islanders*, quoted at the head of this chapter.

If the community at St Michael's Mount was flourishing by the late eighteenth century this was even more true of the town which had come to dominate West Penwith as both a trade and cultural centre; Penzance. Life in Penzance now offered new opportunities to its population, away from the harsh realities of earlier centuries. This was especially true for its leading families, and among these families were counted two that are central to the Brontë story; the Carnes and the Branwells.

Chapter 2

A Man of Enterprising Spirit

'This friend was a merchant, a man of enterprising spirit and undoubted talent, who was somewhat straitened in his mercantile pursuits for want of capital; but generously proposed to give my father a fair share of his profits, if he would only entrust him with what he could spare; and he thought he might safely promise that whatever sum the latter chose to put into his hands, it should bring him in cent per cent. The small patrimony was speedily sold, and the whole of its price was deposited in the hands of the friendly merchant; who as promptly proceeded to ship his cargo, and prepare for his voyage.'

Anne Brontë, *Agnes Grey*

We have seen how the Roman writer Diodorus Sicilus observed how welcoming and cosmopolitan the area around Penzance was, thanks to its trade links and its position within the natural port of Mount's Bay, yet as the centuries progressed it became isolated from much of the rest of Britain and this gave it a distinct character that survives until this day – after all Cornwall is almost an island, with the River Tamar at its eastern edge failing by just four miles to run from the south to north coast thereby cutting off the county completely from the rest of England.

One thing that unites Cornish people of today to their forebears is a pride in the region from which they come. They know, for example, that King Arthur hailed from Cornwall and that Camelot was named thanks to its location near the River Camel, whatever people in other areas that claim to be Arthur's homeland may say! This legacy is marked today by the haunting statue named Gallos near Tintagel Castle. Gallos means 'power' in the Cornish language, and the eight-foot bronze statue is said to represent Merlin holding a sword, although many believe it to be King Arthur himself looking out to sea from the land he once ruled.

Whether King Arthur was real or fictitious we may never know, but Tintagel Castle is just one of many ancient fortifications scattered across Cornwall, timeless reminders of the county's fractious past and fiercely independent nature. We shall see later how one such castle, particularly well known to Elizabeth Branwell, plays a central part in the Brontë story, although most people are completely unaware of it.

Arthurian stories were often told in Elizabeth's childhood, along with Cornwall's other great legend – that of Tristan, the nephew of King Mark of Cornwall who, thanks to a magic potion, falls in love with the King's intended bride Iseult with tragic results. There can be little doubt that the Brontë children would have loved these tales and that they would have heard them from their Aunt Elizabeth. After all, we hear first-hand from Ellen Nussey, the great friend of Charlotte Brontë who was a frequent visitor to Haworth Parsonage, that Elizabeth liked nothing better than talking about the county she came from:

> 'She talked a great deal of her younger days; the gaieties of
> her dear native town Penzance, in Cornwall, the soft, warm
> climate, etc[1].'

Arthur and Tristan have become legendary names across the globe, but of course Guinevere and Iseult have just as big a part to play in their story, and Cornwall as a whole is a county where women played a more prominent role than in many parts of the country. One example from Penzance's history is Alice de Lisle. She was the sister of Lord Henry Tyes, who was the feudal Lord of the Manor of Alverton, encompassing Penzance and the surrounding areas. In 1322, he, like many from Cornwall, took part in a revolt against the unpopular Edward II, but he was captured and executed, along with Alice de Lisle's husband[2]. Lord Tyes' lands were forfeit to the King, but Alice lobbied to have them returned. In 1332 they were given back to her, in effect making Alice Lord of the Manor. Under her leadership Penzance became a leading market town in the area and its influence grew.

Many women of Penzance from less aristocratic stock also, by necessity, took control of their families and property, as their husbands were frequently away at sea, fishing. Fishing remains a major industry in the town, but it held far more importance in previous centuries. Many of those who were not involved in fishing, or in the trade of goods associated with it, found work in the navy and its importance as a strategic naval port led to an incident in 1595 that has been largely forgotten in the annals of British history, even though it was the last invasion on British soil until German troops landed in the Channel Islands during the Second World War. We all know, of course, that the Spanish Armada of 1588, sent with the aim of removing Elizabeth from the throne and restoring England to Catholicism, was foiled by a mixture of bad weather and bad judgement. What is less well-known is that a Spanish army of around 600 troops actually did land in Penzance seven years later, and held the town for two days[3].

Elizabeth Branwell shared an independent spirit and belief in hard work with the wives of Penzance's farmers and fishermen. These, along with piety, were qualities that she prized above all others, and it is thanks to her teachings and example that Charlotte, Emily and Anne succeeded in becoming great writers, against all odds.

The Penzance that Elizabeth and her siblings grew up in was very different to the one that had witnessed the Spanish invasion two centuries earlier. Although they only held the town for two days, the Spanish troops sacked many of its buildings, and this fate was repeated decades later during the English Civil War. The people of Penzance, and indeed of Cornwall as a whole, were predominantly on the king's side, and paid a heavy price for it when the Parliamentarian army under Sir Thomas Fairfax arrived. In May 1648, an event known as the Plunder of Penzance occurred, during which seventy of Penzance's royalists were slaughtered. Nevertheless, the town rose up again in a rebellion called the Gear Rout, eventually put down savagely by the Roundhead leader, Sir Hardress Waller[4].

These dreadful events, exacerbated by the plague that visited the town in 1578, destroyed much of the town's Tudor, and earlier, buildings and significantly reduced the population, but they also increased the fiercely proud and independent nature of its townfolk. The Gear Rout, which at the time seemed so disastrous, actually turned into a propitious event. King Charles II, acceding to the throne after the Restoration of the monarchy in 1660, was aware of how loyally the townsfolk of Penzance had acted in support of his father, and this was behind his decision in 1663 to confer upon Penzance the rank of a coinage town[5].

As a coinage town, Penzance weighed and then collected the taxes due on tin and copper produced in the area. This gave Penzance great prestige, and also increased its wealth. This auspicious combination helped Penzance to grow in size, allowing it to rebuild itself in a grand style from the ruins left behind by the armies of Spain and Sir Thomas Fairfax.

Tin mining was, alongside fishing, the staple industry of Penzance and many of the town's workers fulfilled both roles. Evidence of tin mining in

West Penwith goes back more than 4,000 years, and the area had riches buried beneath the soil that were unparalleled in the rest of Britain. It was this that struck the *Robinson Crusoe* author Daniel Defoe as he reached the westernmost point on his journey across Britain:

> 'Penzance ... is the farthest Town, of any note, West, being 254 miles from London, and within about Ten Miles of the Promontory called the Land's-End; so that this Promontory is from London 264 miles, or thereabouts. This is a Market-town of good Business, well-built and populous, has a good Trade, and a great many Ships belonging to it, notwithstanding it is so remote. Here are also a great many Families of Gentlemen, tho in this utmost Angle of the Nation: and, which is yet more strange, the Veins of Lead, Tin, and Copper Ore, are said to be seen, even to the utmost Extent of Land at Low-water Mark, and in the very Sea. So rich, so valuable a Treasure is contained in these Parts of Great Britain[6].'

Defoe was witnessing the start of a boom period for Penzance, and as the eighteenth century progressed, its mineral deposits were in ever-increasing demand thanks to the Industrial Revolution and its voracious appetite for metals of all kinds. These were halcyon decades for the area's ship industry and for its sailors as well, as the century saw conflict between Britain and France in the Seven Years War between 1756 and 1763.

The population of Penzance was growing, and workers were coming from Ireland and Wales to work its mines. By 1770, the population stood at around 3,000, with many more in the surrounding villages. This led to a growth in the town's market, and an increase in the number of stores serving the population, from grocers to inn-keepers. Some of the most successful merchants, the families of gentlemen referred to by Defoe, had interests in all of these ventures and more, and they increased in wealth and property year by year. One such upwardly mobile unit was the Bramwell family, later to become known as the Branwells. It is widely known that the Brontë name was changed from its original form of Brunty, or even Prunty, by Patrick, possibly to downplay his Irish origins when he arrived at Cambridge University from County Down in 1802. It is less well known that a similar transition happened on the maternal side of the Brontë sisters' family. The spelling of surnames could be fluid in the seventeenth century, when we find records of the Bramble family in Penzance, by the eighteenth century we see them as the Bramwells, and only from Elizabeth's generation onwards does the name settle upon the less bucolic-sounding Branwell.

In 1742, eighteen years after Defoe had travelled through the town, one of its increasingly successful gentlemen, Richard Bramwell, married a woman from another of Penzance's notable families, Margaret John, whose father was the blacksmith, Thomas John. The wedding took place at St Maddern's church in Madron to the north of Penzance, then the official parish church for the area, and they were both 30 years old. This was unusually old for such a match to be made, so it may be that the marriage was one of convenience between representatives of two families of importance. As we shall see, however, they were certainly not only the only members of the extended Branwell family who would marry later in life.

Richard and Margaret had eight children, four sons and four daughters, although two sons named Martin both died in infancy.[7] It was common practice for children to take the name of a deceased brother or sister, and a generation later this was also the reason for Elizabeth Branwell's given name. The surviving sons, Richard and his younger brother Thomas, grew to adulthood and had families of their own, creating a large group of cousins who were among the leaders of Penzance society at the turn of the nineteenth century and beyond. The four sisters were named Margaret, Elizabeth, Jane and Alice. The third daughter Jane is of especial interest to us as she became the favourite aunt of Elizabeth Branwell, and also played a vital role in the Brontë story.

As the two surviving sons of Richard Branwell, Richard junior and Thomas, grew into adulthood so the fortunes of the family grew, but it was the youngest son Thomas in particular who achieved success in the world of commerce. By the time Thomas Bramwell made his will on March 26 1808,[8] he had a property portfolio covering much of Penzance, including shops, a warehouse at the quayside, an inn and brewery, and the largest mansion in the town, Tremenheere House[9]. If these properties had been inherited, rather than earned, then we would have expected them to have been owned by Richard, the older brother, but in fact Thomas was providing Richard with both a job and a home at this time, as the older brother was serving as landlord of Penzance's Golden Lion Inn, owned by his younger brother.

Thomas Branwell, as he came to be known with the 'm' finally exchanged for an 'n', had recognised the potential that the growing town of Penzance offered in the latter half of the eighteenth century, investing in property as well as concentrating on the trade that had been the staple of his family for generation after generation. For a man now rising in society, and growing in wealth and influence as well, there was one thing above all else that was expected of him; to marry and raise a family who would continue to expand the Branwell legacy after he had gone.

With marriage in mind, Thomas was likely to have been encouraged to take the same step that his father had and marry a woman from another of the leading families in Penzance. The woman he chose certainly fitted this description; two years his senior, Anne Carne was the daughter of John and Anne Carne. The Carnes were a large and well-respected family in Penzance, known both for their piety and for their financial acumen. In later years, they were at the forefront of the religious revival taking place in western Cornwall, and the family were also banking pioneers who opened the town's Batten, Carne & Carne Bank in 1797.

Thomas Branwell and Anne Carne married in 1768 in the same Madron church that had seen Thomas' parents Richard and Margaret take their vows twenty-six years earlier. We can conjecture that Thomas and Ann enjoyed a happy marriage, as it was certainly a fruitful one. Over a twenty-year period, they had twelve children together, but like many families in the late-eighteenth century they experienced tragedies as well as moments of happiness and triumph. Doubtless they would have looked to their sons to carry their name forward into the world, just as Patrick and Maria Brontë would later do with their only son, but only one of the Branwell's three sons survived infancy. Little could they have known that it would be two of their daughters who would give their family an immortal legacy, and still less could they have known that in 1975 a plaque would be unveiled at the house they lived in at Chapel Street, Penzance. It reads:

'This was the home of Maria and Elizabeth Branwell, the mother and aunt of Charlotte, Emily, Anne and Branwell Brontë.'

Chapter 3

Fairly Spread Thy Early Sail

'Sometimes I seem to see thee rise,
A glorious child again -
All virtues beaming from thine eyes,
That ever honoured men -
Courage and Truth, a generous breast,
Where Love and Gladness lay;
A being whose very Memory blest,
And made the mourner gay -
O, fairly spread thy early sail,
And fresh and pure and free,
Was the first impulse of the gale,
That urged life's wave for thee!'

Emily Brontë, *E.W. to A.G.A.*

The town of Penzance grew in size and prosperity throughout the latter half of the eighteenth century, although the majority of the population didn't notice much difference in their day-to-day existence. Life as a fisherman or a tin miner was tough and dangerous, bringing with it little security; under these circumstances it is hardly surprising that some of the townsfolk, and those who had been drawn to Penzance in search of a better life, entered into criminal activities from time to time, from the 'wreckers' who would scavenge for goods whenever shipwrecks occurred, to smugglers who took a more proactive approach to the liberation of property and avoidance of tax.

These concerns occupied the thoughts of Thomas Branwell from a moral point of view, but he was free from the financial worries and uncertainty that beset most of the townsfolk. Tradesmen and merchants such as he were presented with a growing number of opportunities, and they also operated in an atmosphere of fraternity and friendship. Trades were passed on from generation to generation, and families married into other families of a similar social standing, cementing further the bonds that united those in the town's business community.

Thomas and Ann had many friends in Penzance and the surrounding area, people whose occupations were butchers, grocers, tea merchants, fish traders, teachers and clergymen. One family well-known to the Branwells were the Tonkins, who lived in Sennen, nine miles to the west, near Land's End. The head of the family, Charles, was a grocer and flour dealer in Penzance, but his children were of a more artistic bent, reflecting the cultural flourishing of the town at the time. His daughter was an acclaimed singer and his sons were musicians, but of most interest is his son James Tonkin, who was born in 1757. As well as being a pianist, James was also a fine artist, painting Cornish landscapes[1] as well as miniature portraits of his friends and acquaintances.

In 1799, James Tonkin painted two individual portraits of Thomas and Anne Branwell, the only confirmed pictures of the parents of Maria and Elizabeth Branwell, and the grandparents of the Brontës. They were then in their mid-fifties. Anne is round-faced and serious, sporting a large white cap with a black ribbon around it and enveloped in a black shawl – the black possibly being a sign of mourning for the loss of her second daughter Margaret, who died in that year. Thomas cuts a very different figure. His stovepipe hat and voluminous neck scarf (the kind that came to be known as a 'Wellington' and that was invariably sported by Patrick Brontë) make him look an archetypal Georgian era gentleman, which is exactly what he was. One thing seems certain when you look at the Branwell portraits, these are a successful couple, a man and woman of substance.

Also noticeable about Thomas Branwell is his long aquiline nose and the faint hint of a smile upon his face. There is certainly a family resemblance to the face on the portrait we have of Maria Brontë, and there is also a similarity to the watercolour portrait of a 13-year-old Anne Brontë, painted by her sister Charlotte. Tonkins painted a series of tiny oval framed portraits of the two branches of the Branwell family in 1799. They are now owned by the Brontë Parsonage Museum, and we have this excellent description of Elizabeth's portrait dating from the year 1937:

'In 1799 Elizabeth was 23 years of age. Her miniature shows a girl with soft brown hair, pale brown eyes, and a serious expression. She wears a pretty white dress with a posy of blue flowers at her breast. She resembles her father and sister Maria, rather than her mother[2].'

There is also a charming silhouette of Elizabeth in the Brontë Parsonage Museum, in which she is clearly wearing a hat and neck ruff very similar to that worn by her mother Anne in her 1799 portrait.

By the time of Thomas' wedding to Anne he had already begun to acquire wealth and property, and his will gives an indication of just how much he possessed by the time he set it down in 1808. We find the aforementioned Golden Lion Inn, being run for him by his older brother – perhaps a strange source of income for a man who had become a devout follower of the Methodist cause that avowed temperance. We also find a fish cellar at the Penzance quay, showing how Thomas had diversified from his family trade of butcher. He owned a malt house at Causeway Head, two houses on Chapel Street, Penzance, along with three other houses in the town, and further houses and land in Leskudjac and Leskinnick[3].

There can be little doubt that Elizabeth Branwell was proud of the success of her parents, and the comfortable childhood that it allowed her to experience, and she related tales of her youth, the opulent balls and social whirl of Penzance society, to her nephew and nieces. This must have seemed a very different world to the Brontë children growing up in a much less luxurious lifestyle on the edge of wind-blasted moors, until in their young minds they magnified still further the wealth and importance of the Cornish grandparents they never had a chance to know.

We get a glimpse of this in the opening to Anne Brontë's first novel *Agnes Grey*. It is a beautiful work of fiction, but it also contains elements that are largely autobiographical; the eponymous heroine is after all a governess who is the daughter of a clergyman in the north of England. Anne, as Agnes, describes how Reverend Grey wed a woman of a much higher social status who made a great sacrifice when marrying him:

> 'My mother, who married him against the wishes of her friends, was a squire's daughter, and a woman of spirit. In vain it was represented to her, that if she became a poor parson's wife, she must relinquish her carriage and her lady's-maid, and all the luxuries and elegance of affluence[4].'

Here we see how Elizabeth's tales of the mother who died when Anne was an infant, and of this mother's own parents, became deeply rooted in Anne's mind and over time became amplified. Nevertheless, given their social standing and wealth, it is certain that Thomas and Anne Branwell would have employed a number of servants, and travelled by carriage. Thomas, of course, was from merchant stock and far removed from a country squire, but in 1788, two years before the death of his father Richard, he did take a step up the social ladder when he was made a town councillor[5].

Happily married, with financial security already in place and a bright future seemingly in front of them, there was only one other thing a late-eighteenth century couple needed; a family. It was a day of celebration, therefore, when Anne Branwell gave birth to her first child in 1769, just a year after they were married. It was a healthy, happy daughter and as was customary at the time, and as was repeated by Maria and Patrick Brontë in the succeeding generation, she was given her mother's name.

As their daughter Anne grew up, her parents must have wondered what the future would hold for her. As a daughter she would not be expected to inherit the Branwell estate (although we shall see how Thomas Branwell was more enlightened than many men of his time in this respect), and nor would she be expected to become a businesswoman in her own right. It would instead be envisaged that she would marry into one of the leading families in the town, perhaps a Carne, a John, a Giddy or a Davy, as her mother had done. They would also have expected their eldest daughter to have taken a role in raising the siblings that would come after her, if she was fortunate enough to make it out of childhood herself.

The early days of Anne's life must have been of particular concern to her parents, as while life expectancy in Cornwall in the late-eighteenth century was around 28 years of age[6], this figure was skewed by two factors – the extremely hazardous nature of tin and copper mining, and the high infant mortality rate. While the Branwell children were immune to the first factor, deaths of children and infants affected families of all classes – as the Branwells would all too soon discover.

Disease was rampant across the south west of England, with outbreaks of typhus, whooping cough and cholera sweeping across Cornwall at regular intervals, removing the old, infirm and young alike. Whilst we do not have official infant mortality figures for Cornwall at this time, the official figures for Haworth in Yorkshire in the middle of the nineteenth century make shocking reading, with 41.6 per cent of the population dying before they reached their sixth birthday[7]. Whilst Haworth was famously unhealthy, largely due to its poor sanitation, it is likely that infant death rates were also high in the Penzance of the previous century. Children in Penzance such as the young Branwells also had an extra threat – the sea. Death by drowning was a reality that many Cornish families had to deal with, not only because of fishermen lost at sea but also because of inquisitive youngsters swept away by sudden waves or cut off by an incoming tide.

The ferocity of the waters around Cornwall reached a head at two o'clock in the afternoon on 1 November 1855, when Penzance was hit by a tsunami. The devastating waves were caused by a huge earthquake that had struck Lisbon in Portugal, some eight hundred miles to the south, earlier that day, and contemporary reports indicate that there was considerable damage to Penzance and the surrounding villages, as well as a significant, although not officially quantified, loss of life. One eye-witness account was given by Reverend William Borlase, a keen amateur scientist and geologist:

> 'The first and second refluxes were not so violent as the 3rd and 4th (tsunami waves) at which time the sea was as rapid as that of a mill-stream descending to an undershot wheel and the rebounds of the sea continued in their full fury for fully 2 hours[8].'

Thomas and Anne, then nine and eleven respectively, must have watched this event with a mixture of terror and awe, similar to that experienced by their grandchildren, Anne, Branwell and Emily Brontë 69 years later when they themselves were nearly enveloped by a seven foot high torrent of mud after an explosion known as a bog burst on the Haworth moorland they were walking through. A local newspaper reported how the explosion could be heard for miles around and also reveals how close it came to claiming the lives of the young Brontës:

> 'Somebody gave alarm, and thereby saved the lives of some children who would otherwise have been swept away[9].'

As Elizabeth Branwell witnessed, with great relief, her nephew and nieces return bedraggled, but safe, to the parsonage on that day in September 1824, her mind must surely have gone back to the stories her parents had told her about the Cornish tsunami, an event that could have seen them swept away too.

In 1770, a year after the birth of Anne, Thomas and Anne Branwell had their second child, another daughter whom they christened Margaret after her grandmother. Like Anne, Margaret Branwell was a healthy child and grew into adulthood (although she died at the age of 29, just as her niece Anne Bronte would do,) but a double tragedy was about to strike the Branwells of Penzance.

1771 saw the birth of their first son, named Thomas after his father, and this was a day of joy and celebration. The two daughters, Anne and Margaret, were loved in their own rights, but here was the son who would become the man to take the Branwell name and businesses into the next century. Alas, it was not to be, and Thomas died within a year. By the time of Thomas Branwell's infant death his mother Anne was pregnant again, and in 1772 her third daughter Elizabeth was born. This is not, however, the Elizabeth Branwell who is remembered by the plaque on Chapel Street in Penzance and not the Elizabeth Branwell who would go on to have so much influence upon the Brontë sisters and their work; no, this Elizabeth Branwell, like her brother Thomas before her, died in infancy in February 1776, at three years old.

Although child mortality was much more common at this time than it is today, and something that most parents experienced at some point, we should not imagine that this made such deaths any less sorrowful, or that it assuaged the grief or feelings of guilt of the parents. Nevertheless, the family of Thomas and Anne Branwell continued to grow. In 1773, another daughter, Jane, arrived and in 1775 she gained a brother named Benjamin. Benjamin was to be the only son of Thomas and Anne who would see adulthood (although he would later, all too briefly, have a brother Thomas who shared the sad fate of his sibling who bore the same name), and he carried the family name with pride, creating his own wealth and obtaining a position at the head of Penzance society. Jane Branwell was destined for a very different kind of life, one where hope was quickly followed by disappointment and sorrow, but it is from her sad story that the Branwell line continues to this day.

As the years passed, the Branwell family continued to grow, and in late November 1776, their seventh child was born; another daughter, they gave her the name borne by the sister who had died just nine months before – this was the Elizabeth Branwell who would one day leave Cornwall for Yorkshire to become a second mother to six needy children and in so doing change the course of literary history.

Elizabeth was baptised at St Maddern's church in Madron on the second of December. Her father was by this time a wealthy and highly respected man, and the leading figures from Penzance and the surrounding towns and villages were in attendance. It was a solemn ceremony conducted in accordance with the traditions of the Church of England, even though her parents were by then supporters of the Wesleyan cause that was growing rapidly in popularity in Cornwall.

Alongside the essential act of a church baptism there was one other rite that the baby Elizabeth had to go through, and it took place not far from St Maddern's church. This was an ancient, and rather strange, ceremony, but one that was still adhered to by families of the region for fear of what could happen otherwise. Around a mile north of Madron's church is a wishing well, today unremarkable and difficult to find, that draws up spring water. In May, traditionally the month of Mary mother of Jesus and therefore particularly auspicious, infants were brought to the well and, naked, were gently lowered into the water until fully immersed as if undergoing a second baptism. After being bathed in Madron Well it was believed that the child was blessed with protection against natural diseases, and just as importantly they would be given holy protection against the evil eye and the unseen yet deadly forces of witchcraft[10].

Now safely baptised in the name of the Father, Son and Holy Spirit, and given the added protection of the waters of Madron Well, Elizabeth Branwell was ready to begin her adventure in life. It was a life that would turn out very differently to how she, or any of her family, could have envisaged it, and yet always at its heart was one word; family. Growing up, she looked up particularly to her eldest sister Anne, seven years her senior. It was Anne who would read bedtime stories to her, Anne who showed her the delights of Penzance, and later Anne who introduced her into Penzance society with all its delights. This role, elder sister, educator, advisor, confidante and best friend, was one that Elizabeth herself would later carry out with great aplomb for her younger sisters Maria and Charlotte.

Elizabeth's childhood in Penzance had moments of loss and sadness, but it also contained delights that stayed with her forever, introducing her to places, people and events she later told her nieces about and that found their way, sometimes disguised, into their work. This was a time when Elizabeth began to show the intellectual ability she became known for, and the kindness, common sense and dependability that proved invaluable to so many people. She had set sail on her voyage through life, a turbulent voyage that would all too soon carry her far away from the Cornwall she knew and loved.

Chapter 4

Blooming and Young and Fair

'The other was a slender girl,
Blooming and young and fair,
The snowy neck was shaded with,
The long bright sunny hair,
And those deep eyes of watery blue,
So sweetly sad they seem'd,
And every feature in her face,
With pensive sorrow teem'd.
The youth beheld her saddened air,
And smiling cheerfully,
He said "How pleasant is the land,
Of sunny Araby!
Zenobia, I never saw,
A lovelier eye than this;
I never felt my spirit raised with more unbroken bliss!..
So pleasant are the scents that rise,
From flowers of loveliest hue,
And more than all – Zenobia,
I am alone with you!"'

Anne Brontë, *Alexander and Zenobia*

At the time of Elizabeth Branwell's birth in 1776, her family were living in a house near to the Penzance quay, with an unspoilt view of Mount's Bay, the island of St Michael's Mount, and the seemingly endless sea stretching away beyond it. It was an endlessly fascinating place for an inquisitive young girl like Elizabeth to grow up in. Woken in the morning by the cry of seagulls, and with the fresh sea air filling her nostrils, she could look out of her window and see, however early it was, fishing vessels setting out in pursuit of a catch, or returning with their nets full of pilchards.

The boats have modernised throughout the years, but fishing had been carried on in a similar fashion in Mount's Bay for century upon century. There was also a more contemporary, and rather less picturesque, industry that met Elizabeth's gaze as she looked along the coastline just to the south of Penzance, for situated there was a subterranean tin mine known as the Huel Wherry. It was opened in 1778, by an industrious miner named Thomas Curtis[1] and was located 240 yards out to sea. Miners had to walk along a plank above the sea to reach the entrance, and a large chimney, billowing smoke, rose 12 feet above the waves. The mine proved highly profitable, but it met an ignominious end in 1798, when it was damaged beyond repair by an American ship drifting in a storm. No doubt this is something that Elizabeth, by that time aged 22, would have discussed with her friends, as it was, after all, the only mine ever to be destroyed by a shipwreck.

The location of the Branwell house near the quay was of course highly convenient for Thomas Branwell, as much of his business was conducted there, and he had his own cellar that held goods later sold at his butcher's shop. Other bonded warehouses lined the quayside, full of everything from fish to tea, and from snuff to brandy, where they waited until they had been assessed for taxation purposes and passed through the Customs House[2]. This made it an ideal place for merchants of all kinds to meet, and it was for this reason that the area around Penzance's quay was the fashionable place to live in the mid-eighteenth century, a time when commerce was beginning to boom.

As a child living near the quay, Elizabeth would have seen and heard a diverse range of people and accents as merchants and sailors from distant lands often landed in Penzance to pick up goods or dispose of their own. She came to know the different types and classes of ships, understood nautical terminology, and looked out towards the sea on particularly stormy nights, hands clasped in silent prayer with her sisters alongside her.

In 1805, a local ship brought mournful news to Penzance, making it the first town in England to hear of the death of Lord Horatio Nelson. The warship HMS *Pickle*, nearing the end of its journey back from the Battle of Trafalgar, told a passing fishing boat of the death-in-action of the great British admiral. There could be no more thought of fishing that day, the boat immediately turned round and sailed back into the port of Penzance. The news was broadcast from the gallery of the Union Hotel on Chapel Street, and an impromptu parade gathered by the quay before marching to Madron church to pay homage. At the head of the parade was the Mayor of Penzance, Thomas Giddy, and his family. Other councillors also took up prominent positions, so we can be sure that Elizabeth Branwell would have marched alongside her father and her siblings, looking with sad solemnity upon the rapidly made banner that proclaimed: 'Mourn for the Brave, the Glorious Nelson gone, His Last Sea Fight is Fought, His Work of Glory Done[3].'

The great reverence for Nelson held by Elizabeth and the people of Penzance was also shared by Patrick Brontë, who hero-worshipped both Nelson and Arthur Wellesley, the Duke of Wellington. It is thought that one of the reasons Patrick adopted the surname of Brontë is that in 1799, King Ferdinand III of the Two Sicilies rewarded Nelson for his services to Europe by giving him Castello Maniace on Sicily and creating him Duke of Brontë, the nearby town[4].

As the century drew on, the leading figures in the world of Penzance commerce and retail expanded and diversified, and many of them moved away from their houses near the quay to quieter surroundings in the centre of the town. Thomas and Anne Branwell and their family joined this exodus too, as although the exact date is unknown we know that by the last years of the eighteenth century they had moved to the home at 25, Chapel Street that bears the commemorative plaque today.

Chapel Street, then, is where Elizabeth Branwell spent her youth and the early part of her womanhood. It is a long and steeply climbing street, providing good practice for when Elizabeth later encountered the similarly inclined Main Street in Haworth, leading from the waterfront through some of the oldest and most picturesque parts of Penzance. The red-brick house in which the Branwell family lived seems unremarkable today, but at the time it was a large and modern residence. Today it stands at the end of a terrace of four houses, but then it was one of three houses, with the middle one now converted into two.

Situated well above sea level, the rear of the house gave a fine view that Elizabeth and the other Branwell children must have loved. The villages of Newlyn and Mousehole could be seen, along with the beautiful fishing hamlet of Gulval, and, always dominating the view and looking even more spectacular from this raised elevation, was St Michael's Mount.

Within easy walking distance on Chapel Street were the Union Hotel, where the solemn news of the killing of Nelson was first relayed, and the historic Turk's Head Inn. Dating from the thirteenth century, it had become a favoured destination for many of the well-to-do in the town and where business deals were often decided by the shake of a hand. Further along Chapel Street was another long-standing inn, the Admiral

Benbow. A favourite haunt of fishermen, it also had a reputation as a place frequented by smugglers. As evidence of this, 2008 building work revealed a tunnel that led from a quayside warehouse, similar to the one used by Thomas Branwell, running underground for 300 metres before surfacing again at the Admiral Benbow, allowing unscrupulous operators to avoid a taxing visit to the Customs House[5].

Also at the rear of the Branwells' new home in Chapel Street was an outbuilding or cottage that Thomas Branwell turned into a schoolhouse. Elizabeth's early lessons would have been given largely by her mother and would have centred around study of the Bible, a basic education in the humanities, and skills that could prove useful in later careers as a governess or a teacher, including needlework and art, for which external tutors may have been hired.

An essential rite of passage during a girl's education was the production of her sampler. This was typically produced by the child at around the age of 9 and demonstrated her skill at needlework. There would be fine detailing stitched around the borders, along with some artistic embellishments, such as flowers, throughout the whole, and at the centre was a hand-stitched verse. The samplers of the Brontë girls are part of the Brontë Parsonage Museum collection, but we also have a description of the sampler made by the young Elizabeth Branwell. It is dated '17th October 17' – although the final two digits were eaten away by a moth we can calculate the likely year to have been 1786. The wording selected and then sewn by Elizabeth is strangely prescient of the impact she would have on the Brontë children:

> 'Charity decent modest kind
> Softens the high and sears the abject mind
> Not soon provoked, She easily forgives,
> And much she suffers, As she much believes,
> Soft peace she brings
> Where ever she arrives,
> She builds our quiet
> As she forms our lives.
> Lays the rough paths of peevish nature even
> And opens in each heart a little heaven[6].'

In many ways, then, the early education that Elizabeth Branwell received, despite coming from a considerably wealthier background, was very similar to that received in the next generation by her nieces. There was also the same expectation of what the future would hold for her, she would either marry a suitable match and become a housewife, or become a governess – in the latter half of the eighteenth century and first half of the nineteenth century there were few other conventional choices for a woman of her class and standing.

The opening of a schoolroom at the back of his house also reveals a similarity between Thomas Branwell of Cornwall and Patrick Brontë of Ireland and Yorkshire, as both obviously believed in the importance of schooling as both an educational and moral tool. Patrick himself had risen from a relatively poor life in County Down to the highly respectable position as a Church of England minister thanks to the power of education. Wherever he went he tried to set up a Sunday School, and in 1832, twelve years after arriving as the curate of Haworth, he opened the newly built school building there[7]. The Haworth school was just down the lane from his parsonage, so Patrick could watch the local children marching to attend it. In just the same way, Thomas Branwell could see the children attending his school, for it was a 'penny school' that he made available to local children at affordable rates, as well as placing his own children there at the appropriate age.

Whilst the former Branwell home on Chapel Street still stands, and is still lived in as a private residence, the school house at its rear was destroyed during a Second World War bombing raid. Nevertheless, we do have a first-hand account of it given by Muriel Beckerleg, who lived in the house before the war and into the 1960s:

> 'The old schoolroom was a delightful place, and as we were a large family it was grand to have our parties there ... it was in grand order. The garden is better without it for now we have a clear view of St Michael's Mount, the Mount's Bay, Newlyn and Mousehole – the fishing villages, and just now there is a wonderfully clear, blue sea and coast line[8].'

Unfortunately, as we do not know the year the Branwell's penny school was opened, we have no way of knowing if Elizabeth attended it or instead completed all of her education at home, but it is certainly possible that some of her education was spent there, and likely that her younger siblings made the short walk from home and entered through its doors. The second Thomas and a sister Alice that came after Elizabeth were both short-lived, but in 1783, seven years after Elizabeth's birth, Maria Branwell was born.

After a further gap of six years, in 1789, Anne, then in her mid-forties, gave birth to her eleventh and final child. Christened Charlotte, she was twenty years younger than her eldest sister Anne. Elizabeth became very close to both these younger sisters, despite a considerable age difference, and she later lived for extended periods with both Maria and Charlotte after they had married.

Once they had received their own education, whether from their mother and private tutors, in the penny school at the rear of their property on Chapel Street, or a mixture of both, the Branwell girls would then have been set to work helping to teach the pupils at their father's school. This provided excellent practice for a future career in teaching, and it also helped to foster a philanthropic community spirit that Thomas and Anne Branwell evidently felt was important. The same path was later taken by the Brontë children, who took turns teaching at the new Haworth Sunday school.

The first undertaking of this duty must have been terrifying to both Branwells and Brontës alike, and we get a remembrance of this in Charlotte Brontë's novel *Shirley* when vicar's niece Caroline Helstone, based on the kind yet shy Anne Brontë, fulfilled her first duties as a Sunday school teacher:

> 'They made her a Sunday-school teacher when she was a little girl of twelve. She is not particularly self-confident by nature, as you may have observed; and the first time she had to 'take a tray', as the phrase is, and make tea in public, there was some piteous trembling and flushing. I observed the speechless panic, the cups shaking in the little hand, and the overflowing teapot filled too full from the urn[9].'

Elizabeth's eldest sister Anne, as might be expected, was the first of the Branwell children to enter employment, but her choice of occupation was something of a surprise for she became not a teacher or a governess but an assistant in a high-quality draper's shop[10]. She was 15 years old, and her decision to seek out a job for herself, and such a job, shows a great degree of self-confidence alongside a longing for independence. It may be that Anne Branwell was inspired by her father's entrepreneurial spirit and commercial successes, and that she dreamed of running her own shop one day, once she had gained first-hand experience of how they operated. Anne's contribution to the shop must have been valued, for she later succeeded in getting her younger sister, Margaret, a job there as well[11].

Thomas recognised a kindred spirit in his first child and approved of it, and we can see her mother's influence in her choice of position as well. Anne junior accompanied her mother to dinners, meetings and soirées in polite society, and learned from her example the importance of keeping up appearances – of being fashionable both in what you wore and in how you furnished and decorated your home. Working in a draper's allowed Anne to indulge this passion for all things fashionable and beautiful.

Elizabeth Branwell was 7 when Anne began her job, a time when she naturally would have looked up to her big sister and been greatly influenced by her thoughts and actions. It is important to remember that whilst Elizabeth became famous for, even mocked for, her old-fashioned clothing in Haworth, with black silk gowns, a large hat and dark shawl her habitual wear, her childhood appearance and mode of dress was very different – as we can see from the portrait James Tonkin made of her in her early twenties.

It is likely, coming as she did under the influence of her older sisters who worked in a draper's shop and living in a well-to-do family who participated fully in Penzance society, that the young Elizabeth would have taken an interest in fashion, but there was one thing she liked even more; books. Novels as an art form were in their infancy in the eighteenth century, and we have only to think of Elizabeth's contemporary Jane Austen's tongue-in-cheek description of Catherine Morland's taste in reading to see what many in polite society of the time thought of women indulging in this activity:

> 'If a rainy morning deprived them of other enjoyments, they were still resolute in meeting in defiance of wet and dirt, and shut themselves up, to read novels together. Yes, novels; - for I will not adopt that ungenerous and impolitic custom so common with novel writers of ... scarcely ever permitting them to be read by their own heroine, who if she accidentally take up a novel, is sure to turn over its insipid pages with disgust[12].'

Both Patrick Brontë and Elizabeth Branwell were avid readers, and both contributed to the library at Haworth, which in turn proved to be very auspicious for the development of the Brontë children, first as readers and then as writers. We know, for instance, that Elizabeth let her nephew and nieces read the periodicals that she subscribed to, including *Fraser's Magazine*, featuring lengthy extracts from works of fiction and non-fiction. This magazine may have been of particular interest to Elizabeth as on occasion it featured works by a man well known to her – her second cousin from Penzance, John Carne[13].

Elizabeth's heart swelled with pride as she gathered her young charges at Haworth Parsonage before her and read to them from her own cousin's work – oh, what it was to have a writer in the family. Especially fascinating to the Brontë children, knowing as we do their childhood love of tales of exploration and adventure in faraway lands, was John's journal of his voyages across the Middle East, which he described in his 1826 work *Letters from the East*. It contains lurid descriptions and fantastical tales that had the young Brontës agog with excitement, including his description of the British explorer and archaeologist Lady Hester Stanhope, niece of former Prime Minister William Pitt the Younger. Frequently crossing hostile territories, she was feted by locals and hailed as 'Zenobia, Queen of Syria' in memory of an earlier Queen:

> 'Her restless and romantic mind dwelt with pleasure on the idea of a power to be established in the East, of which she was to be the mistress: - a large fleet was to come from afar to aid this conquest, and her sceptre was to wave with equal glory to that of Zenobia who defended Palmyra[14].'

This story is likely to have captured the Brontës' imagination, and we can be sure that the name of the heroine did, for Zenobia appears time and again in their juvenilia.

In 1792, death visited Chapel Street, Penzance, as the 23-year-old Anne Branwell sickened and quickly died. This was a great blow to Elizabeth, whose eldest sister had been a constant and loving figure throughout her childhood and youth. Now it was time for Elizabeth to enter womanhood herself, time to explore in full the delights that Penzance could offer – religious delights, cultural delights, delights of the heart.

Chapter 5

Music, Dancing, and Society

'Existence for you must be a scene of continual change and
excitement, or else the world is a dungeon: you must be
admired, you must be courted, you must be flattered – you
must have music, dancing, and society – or you languish, you
die away.'

Charlotte Brontë, *Jane Eyre*

Cornwall may have been all but an island, geographically and
socio-politically, during the years that Elizabeth Branwell grew up there,
but the town of Penzance was certainly not cut off culturally. It was a town
where the divide between the haves and have nots, the thriving merchants
and gentry on one hand and the tin miners, fishermen and smugglers on the
other, was great, but for those on whom fortune smiled there were plenty of
ways to find entertainment or indulge in the arts.

Late-eighteenth century Penzance had its own humane, literary and
scientific societies, and from 1770 it also had a Ladies' Book Club[1],
though it had to wait until 1818 for its first public library. At a time when
books were prohibitively expensive, even for those who had a disposable
income, the book club allowed subscribers access to the latest volumes and
periodicals, as well as providing a forum for them to meet and discuss the
latest scandalous reads away from the censure of their husbands.

Music also played an important part in Penzance life and Elizabeth would
have heard the songs and shanties sung by sailors in port. The tradition
of folk-singing and folk-dancing is still strong in the town, allowing us a
glimpse into the kind of everyday music that must have enchanted Elizabeth
as much as it enchants tourists today. As a Branwell, she also had access to
music of a rather more refined kind as concerts were often held in a room
behind the Turk's Head Inn.

Penzance gained another exciting addition, for those who could afford
it, in 1791 with the opening of the town's own Assembly Rooms in which

balls were often held[2]. Whilst not on the grand scale of the assembly rooms at Bath, so familiar from the works of Jane Austen, they still fulfilled the same primary purpose as a place for the well-off to see and to be seen, a place where respectable people met and shared gossip, and above all where unattached young women could dance with unattached young men, according to strict rules of etiquette, of course, and with a suitable relative in attendance as chaperone.

The Assembly Rooms were built by Elizabeth's uncle, Richard Branwell, and paid for by public subscription, to which we can assume Richard's brother Thomas made a generous contribution. The opulent architecture of the rooms, the beautifully performed music, and above all the heady excitement of a dance, even the anticipation of whether you would be asked to dance, were an intoxicating mix for Elizabeth Branwell, and we know that memories of these days were her favourite topic of conversation throughout the decades she spent in Yorkshire. Balls were held regularly throughout the winter months, the temperate climate of West Penwith making it suitable for this activity and the wearing of finery that inevitably came with it all year round, and Elizabeth attended them in the company of her elder sisters, mother, or her favourite aunt Jane.

Jane Branwell was the sister of Thomas, and was close to him and his children – in more ways than one, as she too lived on Penzance's Chapel Street. Kind and generous to her nephew and nieces, she was also a devout and serious-minded woman, and by the time she had reached her late thirties unmarried it was thought by her acquaintances, if not said to her face, that she would remain a spinster for the rest of her life. Jane, however, had other plans – and their resolution led to a chain of events she could never have envisaged, and for which fans of classic literature across the world can be thankful.

In 1783, a 21-year-old man named John Fennell, originally from Madeley in Shropshire, arrived in Cornwall to take up a position as an assistant schoolmaster in a Penzance school[3]. Cornwall was particularly attractive not only for its spectacular coastline and equitable weather but also because it had become a stronghold of support for Wesleyanism, what we today call Methodism, in which cause he strongly believed.

It was most probably at a Wesleyan meeting that he first met Jane Branwell, for she herself was a committed Methodist, recorded as being an early member of the Penzance Wesleyan Society[4]. Jane was seven years John's senior, but their beliefs were closely aligned, and over bible studies, public lectures and sermons on temperance they fell in love. Jane

Branwell became Mrs. Fennell aged 37 at their wedding on 13 December 1792, at which point they moved to their shared home in Chapel Street where John set up a writing school. Elizabeth and her sisters were frequent visitors to the house of their Uncle John and Aunt Jane, but in 1805 they moved to Shropshire. In 1812, word reached Elizabeth that they had moved even further afield, this time to the West Riding of Yorkshire. She must have thought she would never see her beloved aunt and uncle again, but this supposition proved to be very wrong.

Although Jane Branwell, later Fennell, was the first member of the Branwell family to join the Penzance Wesleyan Society, all of the family became firm adherents to the beliefs and values espoused by John Wesley and his hymn-writing brother Charles. John Wesley was born in 1708 in Lincolnshire and ordained a priest in the Church of England in 1728. Gaining immediate recognition for his great piety and powerful preaching, he founded an association called 'the Holy Club' with his brother Charles and their fellow priest George Whitefield. It was this triumvirate that eventually led to the formation of the Methodist church and its schism from the official Anglican communion, after a long, and at times, dangerous, journey.

John Wesley believed in preaching outdoors, and his doctrine that all people could find redemption in Christ, that no sinner was lost forever, as well as his support for liberal causes such as prison reform, the improvement of conditions for the working class, and the abolition of slavery, won him both friends and enemies in great numbers.

The Methodist Church did not officially split from the Church of England until long after John Wesley's death in 1791, but he was an evangelical maverick at odds with many of the official Anglican doctrines, leading to attempts to suppress him and his supporters. The vicar of Madron, a wealthy landowner named Walter Borlase, was a vociferous opponent of Wesley in his early days, claiming that the preacher was nothing more than an agitator for the Jacobite cause and threatening to have him jailed if he should enter the region again[5]. Undaunted, Wesley found particular support in Cornwall, where his message was welcomed by people whose work was hard and whose lives were often short. He visited the county on a number of occasions, often preaching to huge crowds who had gathered to hear him. There can be no doubt that the Branwells attended these meetings as well, and that Elizabeth, dressed in her finest, would have been amongst the throng during his three addresses to Penzance in the 1780s. By this time Wesley was an old man, but still vigorous in his preaching. The enmity that many had held for him was now gone; even by the time he preached in Penzance in 1860, he had recorded in his journal that, 'at Noon I preached on the cliff near Penzance, where no one now gives an uncivil word[6].'

By the time of John Wesley's death, his rise in fortunes had reached its zenith, and he was acclaimed by many to be 'the best loved man in England and Ireland[7]'. He had preached discipline, that children should obey their parents, that workers should turn away from gambling and drinking, but he had also preached hope and love, and it was a message that resonated across Cornwall and beyond. Certainly, it was a message that Elizabeth Branwell cherished all her life, and one that she imparted to the Brontë children during their Bible reading lessons with her.

The West Riding of Yorkshire was another hotbed of Methodism, and by the time Elizabeth Branwell arrived in Haworth in 1821 it had overtaken the official Church of England in popularity. An ecclesiastical census of 1851, when Patrick was still minister at the Anglican parish church, shows that Haworth's three Methodist churches had 879 in attendance on a Sunday, whereas the Church of England church had only 383[8]. Nevertheless, Elizabeth Branwell dutifully attended the services at St Michael and All Angels' church presided over by her brother-in-law; it was another sign of her constant determination to put family before self, something John Wesley would doubtless have approved of.

Penzance's first Methodist chapel was built on Queen's Street in 1790 and it held up to a thousand people, but Thomas Branwell and others soon saw that this was not large enough to meet the demands of the town's growing Wesleyan community. He became the leading force behind the move to build a new, even larger, Wesleyan church and it was opened on Chapel Street in 1814. The new chapel, still in use today, can accommodate a congregation of 1,350, and it was a day of special pride and honour to the Branwells when it first opened its doors. Sitting in the front pew, Elizabeth looked around with a smile of satisfaction on her face, nodding to the neighbours and acquaintances behind her – unfortunately by then, as we shall see, neither her father nor her mother, who had done so much to bring the building into existence, could be there alongside her to see the fruits of their labours, and even her younger sister Maria was far away.

The large crowds that gathered to see John Wesley and other Methodist preachers, the opening of dedicated Wesleyan chapels, the popularity of Methodist schools, such as the one that John Fennell worked at, all these were signs of the grip that this new evangelical faith had on Penzance in the late-eighteenth century. Another sign was an influx of Methodist priests into the area, one of whom, John Kingston, became particularly well known to Elizabeth Branwell and her family.

The Reverend John Kingston arrived in Penzance in 1799 aged 29[9], and as proof of his missionary zeal he had just returned from seven years as a Methodist preacher in America. John Kingston's own memoir, serialised in *The Methodist Magazine,* describes in great detail his journey to and across North America, and it is clear that at this time he was a very devout and pious man. His religious conversion occurred at the age of 16:

> 'In the sixteenth year of my age, it pleased the Lord, by the ministry of the Methodist Preachers, to convince me of sin, righteousness, and judgement. The thoughts of Death and Eternity filled me with fear. I was burdened with the weight of my misery, and my heart was humbled before the Lord. I withdrew from all my old companions in as decent a manner as I could, and associated with persons of religious character[10].'

Kingston then describes how, after first ministering to inhabitants of London's workhouses he set sail as a missionary in 1791. His first port of call was the West Indies, where he was horrified by the inhumanity of the slave trade:

> 'Presently our eyes were attracted by the horrible sight of a slave ship, which lately arrived from Africa, laden with men and women almost naked. We were penetrated with horror and grief, when we contemplated the situation of these poor wretches, and anticipated the bondage and misery to which accursed avarice had doomed them[11].'

John Kingston's memoirs detail how dangerous this missionary work was for him and for many other Wesleyan preachers at the time, as he survived hurricanes, violent attacks and bouts of the 'black fever' that carried away some of his fellow missionaries. Leaving the Caribbean islands behind, he sailed on to Boston and then New York, where he arrived just in time for an epidemic of yellow fever:

> 'In the month of September, the yellow fever broke out in New York, and raged with great violence, supposed to originate from the intense heat of the weather, and the great influx of

the lower class of people from Domingo. The mortality was so great that sometimes 80 were buried in a day[12].'

These memoirs give us great insight into the minds of a man who would make a significant impact, for better or for worse, on the Branwell family. John Kingston was a man who believed passionately in his Wesleyan faith, and in the common humanity and equality of man. He was a man who faced danger without flinching, and yet he also at times alluded to his own frailties and weaknesses. John returned to Britain in 1798, taking up a post in Haverford West[13], but a year later he made a fateful move to Penzance.

Fired by the missionary zeal that had helped him through his years in America, Kingston was by now an experienced and charismatic preacher. He was also a man of some celebrity within the Wesleyan community, as his arrival in Penzance coincided with the serialisation of his memoirs in *The Methodist Magazine*. These were doubtless read by Elizabeth Branwell and others in her family, and they were filled with excitement at the thought of hearing sermons given by the man who had seen and endured so much for their shared faith.

One member of the family in particular was mesmerised by the tanned, weather-beaten man standing at the pulpit before them – Elizabeth's sister Jane. She was by this time 26 years of age, and although she had met many seemingly eligible young men through her family's social connections, and at dances at the Assembly Rooms, none had caught her interest. Jane dreamed not of a life of steady domesticity in Penzance, becoming the wife of one of the families with whom her father did business, but instead longed for a life of romance and adventure like the heroines of the books she borrowed from the Ladies Reading Club. From the moment she saw John Kingston, Jane knew that was what he offered her – although she could not have guessed how dramatically different her reality would be to her dreams.

1799, the year that John Kingston arrived in Penzance, was a turbulent year for the Branwells. Their fortunes were continuing to rise financially and socially, as evidenced by the series of portraits of the family that James Tonkin was commissioned to paint, but it was also the year that Margaret Fisher, as she had become on marrying Charles Fisher seven years earlier, died. Elizabeth was now the second oldest surviving Branwell daughter, and she was already a figure to look up to for Jane, Benjamin, Maria and Charlotte.

It was in this capacity that Jane, three years her senior, approached Elizabeth one evening in 1799, with the news that she was in love with the town's new Methodist preacher and that she believed her feelings to be reciprocated. This was joyous news to Elizabeth as she thought of her sister Jane following in the footsteps of their aunt of the same name and marrying a man who was an important figure in the local Wesleyan church. Her sister's news would also have brought a tinge of sadness, however, as the life of a Wesleyan minister could be a volatile and itinerant one, and if Jane married Reverend Kingston it was sure to lead her away from her family and into a new life in a new town, or even a new country.

This may also have been on the minds of Thomas and Anne Branwell when they were approached by John Kingston asking for their daughter's hand in marriage. His position within the Wesleyan church, enhanced by his missionary exploits as detailed within *The Methodist Magazine*, should have made him a suitable match for their daughter, and yet Thomas held grave concerns about Kingston's character and his ability to be a good husband for Jane. Nevertheless, within a year of their first meeting, John Kingston and Jane Branwell were married in St Maddern's church on 12 June 1800. Elizabeth, acting as a bridesmaid[14] to the sister who had made her a confidante, envisaged a glorious future for the happy couple and a large family of their own to raise. This last point, at least, would be fulfilled.

Elizabeth saw two sides of Penzance as she grew into her maturity. As the second eldest child of Thomas Branwell she participated in society dinners and events when Jane was unavailable, where she became known both for her kindness and humility. She also saw, however, the other side of Penzance life; the boisterous, alcohol-fuelled life that could be heard ringing through the streets on any evening. Life was hard for the miners and fishermen and many of them, especially those who had left their family life behind, sought solace, or at least an hour or two of oblivion, at the bottom of a bottle.

One of Penzance's most famous sons, Humphry Davy, recalled this side of Penzance in his memoir:

> 'Amongst the middle and higher classes, there was little taste for literature, and still less for science, and their pursuits were rarely of a dignified or intellectual kind. Hunting, shooting, wrestling, cockfighting, generally ending in drunkenness, were what they most delighted in. Smuggling was carried on to a great extent, and drunkenness and a low scale of morals were naturally associated with it[15].'

Humphry Davy was born two years before Elizabeth Branwell and is likely to have known her brother Benjamin. From an early age, his academic and scientific genius were evident, and he went on to write his name in history as the first person to isolate a series of elements including calcium, sodium and potassium, as well as for inventing the safety lamp that was given his name – a device that saved the lives of countless tin, copper and coal miners in Cornwall and indeed throughout the world.

Elizabeth was very proud of this illustrious man from her own home town, and sang his praises to the Brontë children that she helped raise, but it is hardly likely that she would have agreed with his rather jaundiced view of Penzance society. Whilst smuggling and drunkenness was all too common in the town, they were particular targets of the Wesleyan church, and so followers like the Branwells would have eschewed such behaviour.

This is not to say that Elizabeth turned her back on the fun and frivolous side of life in this growing town. From the stories she told when in Haworth, she clearly revelled in the balls and dances she attended, and as she returned to this topic time and again in conversation we have to wonder if there was something, or someone, in particular that made these memories so pleasant to her. She was the respected daughter of one of the town's leading merchants, a man of property and position, and from her portrait we can ascertain that she was not unattractive as a young woman, so it seems natural to question whether Elizabeth had a suitor at some point in her life?

A clue, perhaps, lies in one of the possessions that she brought from Penzance to Haworth in 1821, and which can be seen in the Brontë Parsonage Museum today. It is a beautifully ornate and lacquered dressing case in the then highly fashionable 'Japan' style. Opened up, it contains one long compartment and four smaller compartments, and on the lid are her initials. This was a treasured possession of Elizabeth's, as we shall see when we later come to it in her will, and the inclusion of the initials on top seem to indicate that it had been given as a present to her.

As a thing of beauty, which it still is today over two hundred years after it was crafted, it is entirely plausible that it was given to Elizabeth as a mark of affection by someone who she had grown close to. The early-twentieth century Brontë scholar, C. Mabel Edgerley, after talking to Captain Arthur Branwell, Elizabeth's nephew once removed, opined that it may have been gifted to Elizabeth by her cousin, the dashing naval officer Thomas Branwell, son of her Uncle Richard. She also gave this description of cousin Thomas from his miniature painted as part of the same series that saw Elizabeth herself drawn:

'He looks a merry, bright, young fellow, with his fresh complexion, brown eyes, powdered hair, and his cocked hat and coat with gilt buttons. There is a strong resemblance between Branwell Brontë and him[16].'

This is the sort of man whose recollection would bring a smile to Elizabeth Branwell in later years, to whom her thoughts turned on those dark nights when the wind howled around the Yorkshire parsonage that had become her home, when she was alone and far from the place she loved more than any other.

If Elizabeth Branwell did have a suitor, and if for nothing other than the conventions of the time, it is likely that she did, she never married. There would soon be further marriages within her family, however, and two rapid deaths. The results of these events would separate the Branwell family forever.

Chapter 6

By Sight and Report

'I am now acquainted with all the ladies in my parish, and several in this town too; and many others I know by sight and report; but not one of them will suit me for a companion: in fact there is only one person in the world that will; and that is yourself and I want to know your decision?'

Anne Brontë, *Agnes Grey*

As the new century opened in Penzance, the 23-year-old Elizabeth Branwell looked forward to the years to come with hope and optimism. Her parents were happily married and financially secure, with a growing property empire and a respected place within society. Her sister Jane had found love with a Wesleyan preacher, a love that would be resolved in marriage in that summer of 1800, and she may have anticipated similar happiness for herself and her other sisters Maria and Charlotte.

The dawn was greeted by crowds who waited to see the first rising sun of the nineteenth century. It was a time when the festivities were especially loud and gregarious, and based upon centuries-old Cornish traditions. Turning aside from the alcohol-fuelled over-exuberance, Elizabeth instead devoted herself to another new year tradition, sanding a line on the front doorstep, so a first footer could cross it and bring good luck with them. Before retiring to bed on the last night of the eighteenth century she would have lifted her favourite Bible, flicked through its leaves and placed the forefinger of her right hand on a page without looking down – the passage thus selected would give an indication of the year to come.

The 1800 new year celebrations allowed a moment of reflection and an opportunity for a hard-working populace to forget the everyday stresses and strains in a community-wide revel. This hedonistic spirit was even more apparent on 21 June, when the town celebrated Midsummer in a wild and colourful manner. Midsummer festivities were common across Cornwall, but it was noted that:

> 'In no part of Cornwall, is Midsummer celebrated with more hilarity than Penzance and its neighbourhood; for on the 23rd of June, the young people are all alert in the preparations for their favourite festival[1].'

The 1831 account of these festivities given by William Colenso of Penzance is detailed and illuminating, and fully captures the joyous nature of the event. Even though the drunkenness that was prevalent at these events did not suit Elizabeth's tastes, she would surely have relished the atmosphere of fun and happiness, and the sheer spectacle would have thrilled her. It was a time when the whole town came together, wealthy and poor alike, so we can imagine Elizabeth playing her part alongside her sisters. The 1800 Golowan festival, or Mazey Day as it was also known, would have seemed especially auspicious for the Branwell family, coming as it did just eleven days after the marriage of Jane to John Kingston.

Men and women, boys and girls, some wearing masks but all in their finery, marched through the streets with burning torches held aloft, singing as they went, and burning barrels of tar added to the spectacle. Fireworks burst into the night sky before a dizzying yet intricate finale was enacted:

> 'No sooner are the torches burnt out than the inhabitants of the quay quarter, (a great multitude,) male and female, young, middle-aged, and old, virtuous and vicious, sober and drunk, take hands, and forming a long line, run violently through every street, lane, and alley, crying "an eye, an eye, an eye!" At last they stop suddenly and an eye to this enormous needle being opened, by the last two in the string, (whose clasped hands are elevated and arched) the thread of populace run under and through; and continue to repeat the same, till weariness dissolves the union, and sends them home to bed, which is never till past the hour of midnight[2].'

Mazey Day, with its profusion of flames, alcohol and revelry, was banned for safety reasons for 100 years until it returned to Penzance in 1991. It is once again held annually, and although it is still a spectacular sight it must have been even more exhilarating in Elizabeth Branwell's time. It's easy to imagine Elizabeth clasping her sister Jane, now Mrs. Kingston, to herself at the conclusion of the festivities in 1800, tears of happiness and sorrow running down their cheeks, for they knew they would not celebrate together in that way again.

Jane soon found that being a Wesleyan minister's wife, especially a Wesleyan minister filled with missionary zeal like John Kingston, was not as stable as she may have hoped. The Methodist Conference, as its ruling council was called, frequently assigned its preachers to new parishes, so that in 1801, and with Jane already pregnant with the first of her five children, the Kingstons moved to Truro[3]. This was still within visiting distance for Jane's family, as was Launceston where they settled in 1802, but in 1803 he was sent to Nottingham and then in 1805 to Shrewsbury[4]. Jane was now only reachable via letter, by which means Elizabeth learned of her sister's growing family, but at least she could be sure of the respectable life Jane had entered into, and she knew that she need have no concerns for the future of her elder sister.

Jane was not the only one of Elizabeth's siblings that married and started their own family as the eighteenth century moved into the nineteenth. Benjamin Carne Branwell, her only brother, had married on 25 January 1799, at the Madron church that witnessed so many defining events, happy and sad, in the family's story. Once again, we find Elizabeth taking a central role in the wedding, signing her name as a witness on the marriage register[5]. The fact that Elizabeth was chosen as witness rather than her elder sister Jane shows the high regard she was held in by her family and others, and the reputation she had for dependability.

Benjamin's choice of wife, Mary Batten, was looked upon with delight by his father and mother, for she too came from one of Penzance's leading families. Her father, John Batten, had already served as the town's mayor on three occasions, with two more stints to come, and her brother, another John Batten, was made mayor the year after her marriage to Benjamin[6]. The Batten family was at the heart of Penzance politics and administration, and now that Benjamin Branwell had married into it he too would benefit, thanks no doubt to the encouragement and support of his wife who expected nothing less. Whilst his father Thomas had been delighted to have been made a councillor in 1788, at the age of 42, Benjamin climbed even higher and was himself made mayor of Penzance for the year 1809, aged just 33.

Elizabeth was unsurprised at her brother's elevation, for he had always shown himself as one whose talents matched his ambition. Alongside his roles first as councillor and then as mayor, Benjamin was also a town magistrate, and he had also inherited his father Thomas' mercantile acumen as he proved himself to be an excellent businessman and a successful estate agent.

Benjamin and Mary's first child was born in 1801, and named Thomas after his grandfather. This was Elizabeth's first opportunity to fulfil the role of aunt, as she saw far more of little Thomas than her sister Jane's first child born in Truro, also called Thomas and also born in 1801. In what must have been a tragedy for Benjamin, however, his first son died in infancy just as his two brothers of the same name had done.

By the time Benjamin accepted the mayoral chain and ascended into the highest position in Penzance society in January 1808, he had three further children, all of whom would live into adulthood, Mary, Emma and Benjamin Batten. It was a day of great pride not only for him but also for his sisters Elizabeth, Maria and Charlotte who were looking on as he took up his new role amidst ceremonial pomp.

Full of pride, Elizabeth queued with others in 1809, to welcome the new mayor of Penzance. This was the zenith of her life so far, a life that stretched with such promise before her into a future filled with even greater success and prosperity for the Branwells of Penzance. It was also, however, a day tinged with sadness, for Elizabeth and her family were in the middle of a tragic two year period.

The first sign of things to come came in letters from her sister Jane Kingston in Shropshire. Jane's time in Shrewsbury should have been happy, as it gave her a chance to renew acquaintances with her aunt Jane and uncle John Fennell who were also in the county. None of the letters from Jane Kingston to her family survive, but whilst they were at first guarded in their content they must slowly but surely have taken on a despondent tone.

By 1807, there could be no more hiding the truth – John had committed a grievous offence that led to him facing an ecclesiastical court and dismissal as a Wesleyan minister. The nature of this offence was unspecified, although we shall return to it and the effect it had upon his wife and family later[7]. The letter revealing this terrible downturn in Jane's fortunes was also a blow to her sister Elizabeth; with a naturally sensitive and caring disposition, and wishing, above all other things, happiness for those in her own family, Elizabeth realised the far reaching implications contained within a few short lines. Jane by now had four children, and she was pregnant with a fifth. The nature of her husband's dismissal not only meant a halt to the income they relied upon, it also brought shame upon their name, and it was a shame that would follow them wherever they went, making it impossible for him to become a preacher or minister in England again.

This much was evident to John Kingston as well, and his solution was to return to America – the land he had left nine years earlier, but which he saw as a land of opportunity, and a place where he could find the welcome anonymity that was now lost to him in his homeland's Wesleyan community. The idea of emigration was anathema to Jane; she had after all read and heard of his original journeys across America, and the numerous dangers he had faced. She had no desire to expose her children to such an arduous journey to a country where they would have no other family and where deadly fevers were rife. Given moral support and encouragement, via letter, by her eldest sister Elizabeth, Jane argued fiercely for remaining in England, but eventually she had no option but to follow her husband, and he had decided upon returning to Baltimore, a town he'd grown fond of during his time as a preacher there, as described in his memoir:

> 'The Methodist Society of Baltimore is large and respectable; they are a plain, simple, and truly affectionate people, and I received from them every token of friendship that could possibly be expected[8].'

Back in Penzance, Thomas was dismayed at the plight of his daughter, being taken against her will to a land so far away by a man who had disgraced the religion Thomas held so dear. His opinion of Jane's husband was made evident in his will, written in the year after Jane, John and their children sailed for America. The will specified that Jane, along with the rest of Thomas' children, should receive the generous annuity of £50 per year, but only on condition that it all went to Jane and that not one part of her inheritance could go to her husband[9].

Thomas Branwell made his will on 26 March 1808, and it seems clear that it was made urgently at a time when he knew he was gravely ill. Thomas died on 5 April and was buried three days later. The cause of his death is unknown, but given that he wrote his will just ten days beforehand, we can assume that it was from natural causes, probably a long-standing illness that was reaching its conclusion.

Sitting silently in St Maddern's church on that bleak April morning, Elizabeth knew this was a day that marked the end of her carefree days. She was now 31 years old, but her life up to that point had been spent in the happy security of her father's embrace. Wiping a tear from her eye, she remained strong for her mother's sake, but looking across at the black veiled woman beside her a further pang of anxiety pricked at her heart. Without the presence of her father the world was something less than it had once been, and so she must become something more. Was this the time to find a job for herself? She had, after all, at least some experience of teaching in her late father's penny school. The time would come when she would have to make that decision, when she would have to test herself outside of the safe family surroundings she had always known, but for now she knew that her place was at her mother's side. Whatever private ambitions she held, Elizabeth put them to one side until the time was propitious to examine them again.

For many women at this time, the death of their father would have brought not only grief but the awful spectre of poverty, perhaps even bankruptcy or the dreaded workhouse, but thanks to the recently made will, the Branwell girls were freed from that concern. Thomas had ensured that all his five surviving children would receive an annuity of £50, secured against his many properties. Comparing monetary values from the start of the nineteenth century to today is a difficult task, as after all the people of 200 years ago had no need of money for what we would consider essentials today, such as buying or running a car, annual holidays, and utility bills, so a purely inflationary calculation would greatly underestimate how far the money would go. The specialist website Measuring Worth, however, estimates the actual value of that £50 now to be worth somewhere in the mid-forty thousands[10].

Thomas knew that having this money guaranteed year after year would free his daughters from the financial concerns that affected so many, but it also gave one particular daughter freedom of another kind. Upon receiving news of her father's death and the legacy left to her, along with its stipulation that it would become her property and not, as would have been usual, her husband's, Jane Kingston had a heart-breaking decision to make. She had not taken well to life on the east coast of America, and could see that her husband's fortunes were still on a downward turn. Debarred from seeking a career as a Methodist preacher, even on the other side of the Atlantic, John Kingston had instead become a bookseller, with little success. Jane begged him to let her return to Cornwall with her children, saying that whilst their marriage was irretrievably broken she could at least give their children a better life in England. John would hear none of it; he was the husband after all, and his wife must remain by his side.

The arguments must have been fierce and bitter, for in the end a compromise was reached that was suitable to neither party. In April 1809, she set sail[11] from New York to the country she had pined for, leaving her three oldest children behind with their father. Alongside Jane as she waved what she must have thought was a final goodbye to her sons John and Thomas and her daughter Anne, was her infant daughter Elizabeth Jane Kingston, known as Eliza. Ironically, the only child born in America was the only one who had been allowed to travel with her mother to England.

Jane Kingston returned not only to England, but to Penzance, for she set up home with her daughter at 10, Morrab Place, two streets away from the house of her mother and sisters on Chapel Street. It was highly unusual at this time for a mother to leave her husband in this manner, and she was looked down upon by many, especially those who remembered her wedding just nine years earlier. Elizabeth, however, was not a judgemental woman. Others could scorn and sneer, but Elizabeth offered her elder sister support and understanding. Familial love was always unconditional as far as she was concerned; if a sister was in need, she would be there. Elizabeth never stopped looking out for her unfortunate sister Jane and her niece born in America, as we shall see later in the provisions of her will.

Far from seeing Jane's actions as shameful, as many did, Elizabeth instead saw it as an act of courage that allowed her to save at least one of her children. She did not keep this a closely guarded family secret, but talked openly of it to the Brontë children, explaining the lessons that could be learned from Jane's story. It is clear to me that the prototype of Helen Graham, the titular tenant of Wildfell Hall in Anne Brontë's great novel of 1848, was actually Anne's own Aunt Jane – a woman who had defied conventional norms and refused to stay with a husband who threatened her future and that of her child.

Jane Kingston now had her own home and a brighter future to look forward to, but could the same be said of her sisters? The family home at 25, Chapel Street, along with businesses and other properties once owned by Thomas Branwell, had been left to his elder brother Richard, so there was a real possibility that Thomas' wife and children would have to leave. One possible destination was a house at 17, Clare Street in Penzance, that had been left to his widow, presumably so that Richard could move with his family to Chapel Street. From Richard's own will, however, written in 1811, we see that he had allowed his brother's wife and children to remain in situ, while he persevered at the Golden Lion Inn:

> 'Also... my messuage and Dwelling House in Chapel Street in Penzance aforesaid late in the occupation of my sister in law Anne Branwell and now of her daughters[12].'

Richard's will alludes to a sad event that had happened two years earlier, for Anne had died on 19 December 1809, little more than a year-and-a-half after the death of her husband and just months after the return of her daughter Jane from Baltimore.

The house on Chapel Street that had once been home to a growing family was now occupied by Maria and Charlotte, and at the head of the household their elder sister Elizabeth, all of whom were living off of their annuity in lieu of any employment. It was obvious that things had to change, but the catalysts for this inevitability were two further deaths in the family in 1811 and 1812.

The first of these events was especially tragic, as the Branwells were visited by an event known to so many families of Penzance; a death at sea. Thomas, the third son of Richard and his wife Honour (although Richard also had an illegitimate son from an earlier relationship with a woman named Catherine Veale[13]), had become the pride and joy of the extended Branwell family after entering upon a successful career in the Royal Navy. By 1811, the 33-year-old had risen to the rank of First Lieutenant, but on Christmas Eve of that year he died in the cold winter waters off the Danish coast as his ship HMS *St George* sank in a gale at Nazen near Ringkøbing. Seven-hundred-and-thirty-one of the 738-man crew perished, and the bodies that were carried ashore were buried underneath the sand dunes of Thorsminde, now called 'Dead Men's Dunes'. Over 500 souls were lost on board the HMS *Defence* that also sank in the same storm. Lieutenant Branwell was remembered in the *Navy Chronicle* of 1812, although his name was recorded incorrectly:

> 'The *St George, Defence,* and *Cressey*, kept the North Sea five days, in a dreadful gale from the W.N.W. west and south; but, at length, had to combat with a terrible tempest from the N.W. until they were lost. The following is a list

of the principal officers who were on board the *St George* and *Defence* when those vessels were wrecked – In the *St George* Admiral Reynolds, Captain Guion, Lieutenants Napier, Place, Thompson, Brannel, Dance, Tristram, Riches, and Rogers[14].'

This was a terrible blow to his father Richard, and may have hastened the illness that claimed his life three months later in March 1812. It could also, of course, have been a crushing moment for Elizabeth if it was indeed Thomas who had gifted her the monogrammed dressing box she treasured. If this was the death of a true love, it could help to explain why a woman who would seemingly have been a highly eligible choice of wife for many in Penzance instead remained single for the rest of her days.

The death of their uncle was a momentous occasion in the lives of the three sisters at Chapel Street for it once again threw their future, or at least the future possession of the building they called home, into doubt. This question hung heavily in the air throughout quiet times in the house, until one evening in the spring of 1812, Maria told Elizabeth and Charlotte that she had made a decision; she was going to make her own way in the world, and was about to leave Penzance far behind.

It seems probable that all three sisters had thought of entering upon a career as a teacher or governess, but it was Maria, then approaching her twenty-ninth birthday, who put her plan into action. She knew that her Uncle John and Aunt Jane Fennell had just left Shropshire and journeyed northward again to Yorkshire, where they had opened the Wesleyan Woodhouse Grove School at Rawdon, between Leeds and Bradford. After writing to her uncle and aunt, Maria, who had a reputation for being bright and industrious, was offered a post at the school; it was an offer that was quickly accepted.

Maria's news brought Elizabeth conflicting emotions. She saw the sense in her sister's move, and it was one that she herself was thinking of taking – after all, now their uncle was dead, their tenancy of the Chapel Street house was no longer assured. Parting from a sister she had been so close to, however, brought further grief on top of the succession of family bereavements she had suffered in the preceding years. Above all, why did Maria have to travel so far? It was a distance of more than 400 miles, and took around ten days to cover if taken in a carriage. The alternative method of travel, sailing around Wales to Liverpool and then taking a coach to

Rawdon, was almost as arduous. Elizabeth could hardly imagine such a long journey, and even less could she imagine that it was a journey she herself would later make on three occasions.

There was, however, the reassurance of Maria's impending reunion with the aunt they all knew and loved, and their brother Benjamin also spoke up in defence of Maria's plan, as he had already made journeys of similar lengths. Benjamin was not only a successful businessman, he was also a very devout Methodist and a keen theologian who had travelled to Yorkshire in the course of his studies. In the nineteenth century, the Bronte scholar, William Scruton, even suggested that Benjamin may have met Patrick Brontë in Yorkshire prior to 1812, and that he may have had his sister Maria with him at that time[15]. Given the time and money involved in such a journey, however, this seems an unlikely supposition.

What we know for sure is that Maria arrived at Woodhouse Grove School in the early summer of 1812. She was given an administrative role by her Uncle and Aunt Fennell, a role that was also being filled by their daughter Jane. It seems likely that Maria may have expected to step into a teaching role at a later date as the number of pupils increased. Maria found herself 400 miles from the family she had been inseparable from all her life, but this brought a new-found freedom. It was a time of great personal growth for her; previously she had been studious and reserved, but now she could experience aspects of life that had previously escaped her: such as love.

When John Fennell arrived in the West Riding of Yorkshire, he found to his pleasure that in the vicinity were two priests with whom he had become friends in Shropshire; the Welshman William Morgan and the Irishman Patrick Brontë, who had both made the same journey to Yorkshire, an area whose rapidly expanding population were being evangelised by the Wesleyan movement. Knowing their talents and their good nature, Fennell also engaged their services for his school.

Patrick was taken on as an examiner in the classics, a position he was eminently suited for as he was well versed in Greek and Latin from his time as a student at Cambridge University. He soon found his attention drifting away from Virgil and Horace, however, and onto Fennell's niece Maria.

On the face of it, it seems that Patrick and Maria had little in common. She was then in her late-twenties while he was in his mid-thirties, and she was from a relatively wealthy background whereas Patrick was from very humble origins in Drumballyroney, County Down. Indeed, only his intellectual ability, evident from an early age, saved him from the life of a poor farmer, as the local landowner, Reverend Thomas Tighe, subsidised Patrick's entry into Cambridge and then into the Church of England[16]. Patrick had become an eccentric, sometimes irascible, and yet pious and kindly man, and Maria recognised in him a kindred spirit: here they were, a man and a woman perhaps past the prime of their lives and many hundreds of miles from the lands they had called home. His poor background mattered not to Maria, in fact it may have been to his advantage as she had earlier written a pamphlet entitled, *The Advantages of Poverty in Religious Concerns*[17].

A mutual affection quickly changed into true love, and we have seven letters from Maria during this courtship that bear testimony to the strength of their feelings. Patrick is no longer Reverend Brontë, he is Maria's 'Saucy Pat', and on another occasion, she teases him mercilessly by stating that her aunt and uncle thought he was 'mazed' and that even she worried that his lovestruck behaviour had 'the mark of insanity'. In a letter of 23 September 1812, we see a very tender side of their relationship, as Maria writes:

> 'Your joys and sorrows must be mine. Thus shall the one be increased, and the other diminished... and may we feel every trial and distress, for such must be our lot at times, bind us nearer to God and to each other! ... Oh, what sacred pleasure there is in the idea of spending an eternity together in perfect and uninterrupted bliss![18]'

By this time Maria Branwell and Patrick Brontë had known each other for less than three months, but they had already realised that they wanted to marry, and by the end of the year their wish was fulfilled. Eros shot two arrows in the corridors of Woodhouse Grove School that summer, for the Reverend William Morgan had fallen in love with Jane, Maria's cousin. The date of 29 December 1812, was set for their double wedding at St Oswald's church in Guiseley, and the doubly happy event was reported in the *Gentleman's Magazine* at the beginning of 1813:

> 'Lately at Guiseley, near Bradford, by the Rev. William Morgan, minister of Bierley, Rev. P. Brontë, B.A., minister of Hartshead-cum-Clifton, to Maria, third daughter of the late T. Branwell, Esq., of Penzance. At the same time, by the Rev. P. Brontë, Rev. W. Morgan, to the only daughter

of Mr. John Fennell, Headmaster of the Wesleyan Academy near Bradford[19].'

The story of the double wedding is well known, but in fact it was a triple wedding within the Branwell family, thanks to a further wedding at exactly the same time being held more than four miles away, and one of the orchestrators of this rare and precious event was Elizabeth Branwell.

Maria Branwell was an avid and excellent letter writer, as we see from her missives to Pat, so it is without doubt that she wrote to Elizabeth in Penzance to tell her of her new found love. Elizabeth was delighted by this surprising turn of events, but she had a similar story developing within her own home. By mid-1812, only Elizabeth and her 22-year-old sister, Charlotte, were living in Chapel Street, although they had their brother Benjamin and sister Jane nearby. Elizabeth witnessed a growing love between Charlotte and their cousin Joseph Branwell, another son of Richard, and it was clear that their intentions too were to marry. A series of letters then passed between Elizabeth and Charlotte in Penzance, and their sister Maria and cousin Jane in Rawdon, resulting in the simultaneous triple weddings. This was carefully planned, as revealed many years later in a letter to a newspaper from another Charlotte Branwell, the daughter of Charlotte and Joseph and Elizabeth's niece:

'It was arranged that the two marriages [Patrick and Maria and William and Jane] should be solemnised on the same day as that of Miss Charlotte Branwell's mother, fixed for 29th December in far off Penzance. And so, whilst the youngest sister of Mrs. Brontë was being married to her cousin, the late Mr Joseph Branwell, the double marriage, as already noted was taking place in Yorkshire. Miss Charlotte Branwell also adds that at Guiseley not only did the Rev. Mr Brontë and the Rev. Mr Morgan perform the marriage ceremony for one another, but the brides acted as bridesmaids for each other. Mr Fennell, who was a clergyman of the Church of England, would have united the young people, but he had to give both brides away. Miss Branwell notes these facts to prove that the arrangement for the three marriages on the same day was no caprice or eccentricity on the part of Mr Brontë, but was made entirely by the brides. She has many a time heard her mother speak of the circumstances. "It is but seldom," continues

Miss Branwell, "that two sisters and four cousins are united in holy matrimony on the same day[20]."'

Elizabeth acted as bridesmaid for Charlotte, and once again signed her name as a witness at St Maddern's church. It was a joyous day, but now, aged 36, only she remained unmarried of the Branwell siblings, and her future was more uncertain than ever.

Chapter 7

Weary Wandering

'Thou art gone but I am here,
Left behind and mourning on,
Doomed in Dreams to deem thee near,
But to awake and find thee gone!
Ever parted! Broken hearted!
Weary wandering all alone!'

Branwell Brontë, *Song*

The dawn of 1813 saw Maria Brontë and Charlotte Branwell, who had kept hold of her maiden name by dint of marrying a cousin, begin new lives with their husbands, and it also brought a change of location for their sister, Elizabeth. Charlotte, of course, took up residence with her husband Joseph, but it was impractical for Elizabeth to continue living at 25, Chapel Street on her own, and the death of Joseph's father, Richard, who had allowed them to continue living in the home his brother Thomas had bequeathed him, left her with no choice but to move out herself.

Her thoughts may have turned to seeking a position as a governess or teacher, following in her younger sister Maria's footsteps, but if she did attempt to secure such a job she must have been unsuccessful. It seems most likely that Elizabeth moved in to the house that Charlotte and Joseph now occupied[1], presumably the property in the neighbouring village of Gulval where Joseph lived prior to his wedding[2], although it is also possible that she also spent some time with her sister Jane and niece Eliza in Morab Place. The presence of Elizabeth would have been beneficial to Charlotte and Joseph as they looked to start a family. Charlotte could attest to her sister's common sense and practicality; after all, at fourteen years her senior, Elizabeth had been almost a mother figure to her, and as Joseph was holding down a job, a maiden aunt would be able to help with the upbringing of their future children.

It is less likely that Elizabeth would have moved in to the home of her brother Benjamin and his wife Mary, for by this time they already had three children with the likelihood of more to come. Benjamin felt his house was already crowded at this time, for he later bought the house at 25, Chapel Street that had once belonged to his father and removed there with his wife and daughters[2].

Benjamin had not only his father's business acumen but also his sense of philanthropy, and he reopened the penny school at the rear of the house. The school was later taken over by his daughters Mary, Emma and Amelia Josepha, but his third daughter Lydia, born in 1811, was too shy to undertake work of any kind and although she lived into her sixties she 'remained unmarried and was entirely reclusive[3].'

Lydia Branwell was evidently of a similar character to her cousin Emily Brontë. We shall read later how Charlotte and Anne had hoped that Emily would join them as a teacher at their own school, but they eventually had to concede defeat, as revealed in a letter from Charlotte to her former tutor, and object of affection, Constantin Heger:

> 'Emily does not like teaching much, but she would always do the housekeeping and, although she is a little reclusive, she has too good a heart not to do everything for the wellbeing of the children[4].'

Lodging with her sister and new husband, Elizabeth would have found the young couple frequently turning to her for advice and practical assistance, for Joseph, like Charlotte, was thirteen years younger than her. He was Richard Branwell's youngest child, and after completing his education, he decided to put his learning to good use and become a teacher at a school in Queen's Street, Penzance. By the time of his marriage at the end of 1812, however, he had become disillusioned with this choice of career and instead entered a profession more suited to the son of a Branwell by taking a position at Bolitho's Bank, founded in Penzance in 1806 by William Bolitho and Thomas Bolitho the younger. Joseph wasted little time in persuading members of his family to transfer their allegiance and funds to this bank, for the sums awarded by Elizabeth Branwell in her will were still held at Bolitho's.

A full-length silhouette of Joseph shows a slim man of good stature, with a pronounced Roman nose rather reminiscent of that of his nephew Branwell Brontë. He is wearing a frock coat and, most noticeably, is carrying a thin walking cane that seems more fashionable than practical. We are left in little doubt that here is a successful gentleman, and a man to be reckoned with.

Joseph was also a family man, for almost a year to the day after they were married the first of his ten children with Charlotte was born. Elizabeth was delighted to see her youngest sister blessed with a healthy son, named Joseph after his father, but her mind also turned to the sister who, although hundreds of miles away, was always in her thoughts – would she too have children, and if so would Elizabeth ever see them?

Further happy news arrived in Cornwall via a letter from Yorkshire. Carefully opening the envelope, Elizabeth had a premonition of what it would contain; her sister Maria was delighted to announce that she was now expecting a child with her husband Patrick. This was an anxious moment for the married couple at a time when it was far from certain that a pregnancy would lead to a healthy birth. It was an anxiety shared by Elizabeth too who, unable to be with her sister at this juncture as she would have wished, instead had to wait weeks between letters for the latest update. The letter that arrived in the late spring of 1814 was opened by slightly shaking hands, and Elizabeth's heart raced as she scanned quickly through her sister's handwriting to find the news she was looking for; it was good news, for on 23 April 1814, she had given birth to a daughter who would share her name, Maria Brontë.

Maria and Patrick were enjoying a perfect start to their married life. They were living in rented accommodation in a cottage at Lousy Thorn Farm in the village of Hartshead-cum-Clifton on the edge of Mirfield, a centre of the heavy woollen district that lay between Huddersfield and Leeds. Patrick was priest at the village's St Peter's church, and he was widely respected by his parishioners.

Having married rapidly after a brief courtship, Maria was continually learning about her husband, but she found that what she learned was to his credit. His piety was clear for all to see, and yet he also had an artistic and poetic side. In the year following their marriage he published his second collection of poetry entitled *The Rural Minstrel*. Within the collection is a long poem entitled 'Kirkstall Abbey'; it is a tender tribute not only to the magnificent ruined abbey near Leeds but also by implication to his new wife Maria, for it was at Kirkstall Abbey that he had proposed to her in 1812[5].

The life Maria was now settling into was very different to the one she had known in Penzance. There were no dinner parties, no social dances, not even any traditional festivities to brighten a summer evening as she had become used to in Cornwall. The parishioners were hard working and honest folk, but there was also a real sense of danger and unrest in the air. The area around Hartshead was at the centre of the new wool processing industry, and as she looked down from her home high up in the hills she could see a number of factories belching black smoke along the valley bottom. This was the height of the industrial revolution, and traditional jobs were now being performed by machines, so that many found themselves out of work and with no means of supporting themselves or their families. Poverty, starvation and death could come at any time, and many men from the area took the law into their own hands by becoming Luddites.

Luddite campaigns consisted of smashing machines and intimidating mill owners, and Patrick and Maria discovered that they had many of that persuasion in their congregation. Reverend Brontë had seen enough proof of this when a large group of Luddites marched past Lousy Thorn Farm on 11 April 1812 to a meeting point on Hartshead moor known as Dumb Steeple. That night, they attacked Rawfold's Mill and a pitched battle occurred that left some of the Luddites dead and others arrested and facing transportation or hanging. It is said that Patrick turned a blind eye to some of the slain Luddites being buried surreptitiously in his churchyard[6]. We can say without doubt that he later told the story of what must have been a terrible, yet exciting, night to his children, for it is recreated with a little artistic license as a pivotal scene in Charlotte Brontë's *Shirley*:

> 'All the copse up the Hollow was shady and dewy, the hill at its head was green: but just here, in the centre of the sweet glen, Discord, broken loose in the night from control, had beaten the ground with his stamping hoofs, and left it waste and pulverised. The mill yawned all ruinous with unglazed frames; the yard was thickly bestrewn with stones and brickbats; and close under the mill, with the glittering fragments of the shattered windows, muskets and other weapons lay here and there. More than one deep crimson stain was visible on the gravel, a human body lay quiet on its face near the gates, and five or six wounded men writhed and moaned in the bloody dust[7].'

Maria may well have thought this was far from an ideal place to raise a child, and the accommodation she and Patrick were renting was placing a strain on their finances. These problems became more pressing in February 1815, for it was then that their second child, another daughter, was born. Providence smiled on the Brontë family at this point, for Patrick was offered the curacy of the parish of Thornton, near Bradford, which came with the invaluable addition of its own rent-free parsonage. The incumbent minister of Thornton, Thomas Atkinson, had fallen in love with Frances Walker of Lascelles Hall near Huddersfield, 5 miles to the south of Hartshead-cum-Clifton. An agreement was made between the two ministers, after consulting their Bishop, that they would swap parishes[8]; Patrick gained a new home for his growing family, and Thomas was now able to court Frances, who he later married.

Whilst the exchange was agreed in March 1815, the actual move did not take place until 15 May 1815, but when Patrick and Maria arrived in Thornton with their two daughters there was another member of the family alongside them; one who had travelled hundreds of miles to be there.

The letter that Elizabeth Branwell opened in March 1815, brought the welcome news that Maria had successfully given birth to her second child, but it also brought much more. Firstly, there was the revelation that they had decided to name their second daughter Elizabeth in honour of her aunt. This would have brought a happy swell of pride, but tinged with sadness as well at the realisation that this was a niece she would never see; reading further, however, she was presented with an opportunity to do just that.

Maria had explained that there were plans afoot to move to a new parish and a larger house in Thornton, and this allowed them to extend an invitation to Elizabeth to visit them, and also to be a godmother to their new daughter. Tears welled in Elizabeth's eyes as she placed the letter carefully back into its envelope, but how should she respond? There was nothing she would like more than seeing her favourite sister Maria again, for while she was grateful to Charlotte and Benjamin for letting her live with them, the age gap prevented them from ever being close confidantes as she was with Maria. She was also thrilled to be asked to be a godmother to a niece who would bear her own name, especially as by now she must have known that she herself would never marry and have children.

Elizabeth's intuitive response was to accept the invitation, but she was above all else a practical woman, and she also knew the logistical difficulties a journey of this kind presented. Whether travelling by road or sea, it was a long and potentially dangerous undertaking; such journeys were usually only taken as an absolute necessity, and some who did take them wrote out a will beforehand[9].

Elizabeth already had first-hand knowledge of the trouble that such a journey could bring. Shortly after Maria's arrival in Yorkshire in 1812, she had written to Elizabeth asking her to send a selection of her goods after her. Acting on her instructions, Maria's property was carefully packed into a large case that was then sent by sea to Liverpool, after which it would be transported over land to rejoin Maria at Woodhouse Grove. A letter sent by Maria to her beau Patrick a month before they married confirms what happened next:

'I mentioned having sent for my books, clothes, etc. On Saturday evening about the time you were writing the description of your imaginary shipwreck, I was reading and feeling the effects of a real one, having then received a letter from my sister giving me an account of the vessel in which she had sent my box being stranded upon the coast of Devonshire, in consequence of which the box was dashed to pieces with the violence of the sea, and all my little property, with the exception of a very few articles, being swallowed up by the mighty deep[10].'

It is telling that Maria places her books before her clothing and other property in order of importance. One of the books that did survive the disaster was *The Remains of Henry Kirk White* by Robert Southey, published by Vernor, Hood and Sharpe in 1810. White was a deeply pious poet whose tragic life ended aged just 21. Maria Branwell was clearly a great fan of his; rescued from 'the mighty deep' it was purchased from a private collection in 2016, by the Brontë Parsonage Museum for the mighty sum of £200,000[11].

Elizabeth was doubtless mortified at the shipwreck near the Devon coast, not only for the irretrievable loss it occasioned her sister but also for the memories of the death of Lieutenant Thomas Branwell it brought back. Memories of both these events also played upon her mind as she contemplated visiting her sister in Yorkshire in 1815, but the call of family was too strong to resist, and she arrived in the West Riding in time to help the Brontë family move from Hartshead-cum-Clifton to Thornton.

Elizabeth's delight at seeing Maria again was reciprocated by her sister, and she was instantly aware that the three years since she had last seen her had wrought a lot of changes. Gone was the quiet, studious young woman she had known, and in her place was a confident woman whose main concern was her children rather than the latest news and poetry. Her first meeting with her brother-in-law Patrick was a happy one. True, he was older than her sister, although a year younger than Elizabeth, but he was tolerably handsome. It was obvious too that he was a serious, pious man, and these were qualities that Elizabeth prized in a clergyman. Even though he was a solid Anglican rather than a Wesleyan, it was also reassuringly obvious that he was a different breed altogether than the minister her sister Jane had wed.

It had been agreed, in light of the arduous nature of the journey, that Elizabeth would stay with Maria and Patrick for a year, and in this time, they found her an invaluable help in the organisation of their new household and in helping to look after their two daughters. The baby Elizabeth in particular was doted upon by her aunt, as she looked forward with joyful expectation to the day that she would become her godmother.

The parsonage at Market Street, Thornton was very different to the homes Elizabeth had been used to in Penzance. There was no sea view here, of course, but its elevated position instead gave a view to moorland stretching into the distance. It was a sight that would become very familiar to her both in Thornton and later in Haworth, but it seemed achingly dull compared to the coastal vistas she had known. Upon opening the curtains in her room in the morning, Elizabeth was greeted not by the sight of St Michael's Mount but by a strange angular building that, owing to its shape, had become known as the 'coffin end'. Serving as an inn, it is said that the building sometimes organised wrestling matches between men and bears[12].

The parsonage at Thornton has today been lovingly restored and sympathetically extended, but although it was only thirteen years old when the Brontës and Elizabeth moved in, Patrick found it to be a 'very ill-constructed[13]' building, and he frequently had to pay for repairs to be undertaken. Although offering more room and comfort than Lousy Thorn Farm, it was also far from spacious, and this became even more apparent before Elizabeth's departure in 1816, as there was another arrival in the family, and the presence of a new servant: a 13-year-old graduate of the Bradford School of Industry for Girls, named Nancy Garrs.

Elizabeth's room was far less luxurious than she was used to; the local customs, not to mention the accents, confused her; the scenery oppressed her; and worse than all that was the Yorkshire weather, which was a far cry from the temperate climate she'd left behind; and yet she was very happy in Thornton. She was once more in the company of the sister she adored, she had two infants to care for, and she also found there was pleasant society to mix in, thanks to the Firth family of nearby Kipping House.

The Firths were the leading family of Thornton, and Kipping House itself, a short walk downhill from Thornton Parsonage, dated back to the seventeenth century. In May 1815, it was occupied by the widowed Dr John Firth and his 18-year-old daughter, Elizabeth, although in September of that year he married his second wife Anne. They were keen supporters of the Church of England, and so did all they could to make the Brontës, and their guest Elizabeth, welcome.

They soon became firm friends, as we can see from the journal kept by Elizabeth Firth, now housed in the Sheffield University archives, gifted to them by a grandson of Elizabeth Firth who became a Professor at the University. There are details of dinner parties, visits and shopping trips, and on 12 June 1815, we get the first mention of Elizabeth Branwell in the typically terse statement:

'Mrs Brontë and Miss Branwell called[14].'

The diary also reveals that the two sisters, Elizabeth and Maria, had an active social life at this time, as evidenced in this entry for 21 August 1815:

'Mrs Brontë, Miss Branwell and I drank tea at Mr John Ibbotson's[15].'

Five days later an event of altogether greater significance is included in Miss Firth's diary:

'Mr Brontë's daughter was christened Elizabeth by Mr Fennell. My Papa was Godfather, Miss Branwell and I were Godmothers[16].'

This day, 26 August 1815, was one of pure joy for Elizabeth Branwell. She was far away from home in the church of St James, Thornton, but in her arms was a baby she had been entrusted to protect and care for. The vows she took were said with solemnity yet passion, and they were not words she would ever willingly forget or turn her back on. Surely this child,

Elizabeth, waving her arms in the air towards her godmother, would grow into a happy and successful woman? It was a day of contagious smiles as Maria and Patrick beamed with joy, and nearby was Elizabeth's Aunt Jane and her cousin of the same name, with her Uncle John having conducted the ceremony. This little corner of Yorkshire had, for a brief moment, become a part of West Penwith as the Branwell family welcomed another member to their fold. All the protagonists of the 1812 double wedding in Guiseley were here, but this time Elizabeth was the guest of honour among them.

The reason for the half-year gap between the birth of Elizabeth Brontë and her christening will have to remain a mystery, although the move from Hartshead to Thornton may have contributed to the delay. By the time Elizabeth was baptised by the font in her father's church, her mother was already expecting her third baby.

Elizabeth Branwell was still in Thornton on 21 April 1816, when Maria's third child was born, and she probably assisted in the delivery of it in the Thornton parsonage where they lived. Maria kept up the Branwell family tradition of having predominantly daughters, and it was decided to call this third one Charlotte after her aunt in Cornwall, a move Elizabeth wholeheartedly approved of. The choice was appreciated in Penzance too, for in the following year Charlotte and Joseph Branwell gave their newborn son Thomas the middle name of 'Brontë', surely as a mark of thanks for the name given by the Brontës to their daughter.

Elizabeth's stay in Thornton was drawing to an end; the seas of Penzance were calling her home, but we know that it was with great regret that she left her sister and three nieces. Once again, we turn to Elizabeth Firth's diary, as on 28 July 1816, in an unusually fulsome note, she records:

> 'I took leave of Miss Branwell, she kissed me and was much affected. She left Thornton that evening[17].

This sentence is very revealing of Elizabeth's character and of her time in Thornton. She had clearly grown very fond of Elizabeth Firth, and was bereft at the thought of leaving her own family behind in Yorkshire. She had been in Thornton for fourteen months, but must now have assumed that she would never see her sister or nieces again. We also know how much Elizabeth had contributed to the Brontë family during this transitional time for them, and how much it was appreciated, thanks to a present that Patrick gave Elizabeth a few months prior to her departure. It was a copy of his own book of poems, *The Rural Minstrel*, but whilst the choice of gift may not have been ideal, the inscription within it was heartfelt:

> 'Gift of the author to his beloved sister Miss Branwell as a small token of affection and esteem. Thornton nr Bradford. March 29 1816[18].'

It is likely that she called upon the Fennells, now in Bradford, before returning to Penzance, after which the only contact she had with Maria was once again by post. All too soon a letter arrived that would force Elizabeth to make a terrible choice: to turn her back on the place she loved, or on the sister she loved.

Chapter 8

Heart-rending Cries

'Can there be any anguish equal to that occasioned by objects, dear as your own soul, famishing with cold and hunger? Is it not an evil to hear the heart-rending cries of your children craving for that which you have it not in your power to give them? And, as an aggravation of this distress, to know that some are surfeited by abundance at the same time that you and yours are perishing for want?'

Maria Brontë, *The Advantages of Poverty in Religious Concerns*

Elizabeth Branwell arrived back in Cornwall as the autumn of 1816 was dawning, but even so she found the temperature much warmer than she had known in the previous year, as even the Bradford summers were frequently cool and damp. Just as warm was the greeting she received from her sister Charlotte, especially when she gave her news of the niece in Yorkshire who now bore her name.

Elizabeth soon found that life went on in Penzance and Gulval much as it had before. She could once more sit in the family pew at the Wesleyan church her father had helped build, rather than attending Church of England services as she'd had to in Thornton. The sights, sounds, and above all, smells of the sea were to her like the embrace of an old friend. Once more she heard the familiar Cornish burr, discussing storms and catches, there were concerts to attend, and the series of lectures given every winter to occupy the dark nights, even the sound of revellers at the Union Hotel and Admiral Benbow seemed comforting, and yet something was missing. The fourteen months in Thornton had profoundly changed Elizabeth Branwell; the memories of the family living in the small, run-down parsonage in Thornton would not go away.

Letters, at least, continued to arrive from the West Riding, and they brought with them news of a succession of happy events. The opening of such a letter was a grand event, with Charlotte and her children sitting before Elizabeth as she shared their contents and revealed how the family in Yorkshire continued to grow. The epistle that arrived in the summer of 1817 must have seemed especially auspicious, as it announced the arrival of a fourth child for Maria and Patrick, and this time, God be praised, a son. Christened Patrick Branwell Brontë he would forever be known within his family by the middle name that heralded his Cornish roots. Here at last was a boy who would take his family name forward into the world; minister, soldier, engineer, who knew what he might grow into?

The following year brought news from Thornton of a fifth child, a daughter named Emily Jane. There were three Janes within the family who could have influenced the middle name: Aunt Jane Fennell; her daughter Jane who had been wed alongside Maria; or Maria's sister Jane who had married so disastrously. The choice of first name is a little more confusing, as Emily is the only Brontë child not to have been given the first name of a parent or relative; it has to be assumed that it was the name of a friend now unknown.

There was no child in 1819, although Maria's letters did announce that she was pregnant again, along with news that Patrick had been nominated to the curacy of the parish of Haworth, 6 miles from Thornton, a position that brought more money, a larger parsonage building, and more prestige as the celebrated eighteenth century Wesleyan minister William Grimshaw had served as priest there for over twenty years.

Patrick was informed of this nomination in May 1819, via a letter from Reverend Henry Heap[1]. As Vicar of Bradford, the parish of Haworth was his to dispose of as he chose, or so he thought. Unfortunately, he had not taken account of a long-standing, and legally supported, tradition in Haworth that the parish council would nominate their own priest. By the following month the stand-off that developed was already being reported in the Leeds newspapers:

> 'We hear that the Rev. P. Brontë, curate of Thornton, has been nominated by the vicar of Bradford, to the valuable perpetual curacy of Haworth, vacated by the death of the Rev. James Charnock; but that the inhabitants of the chapelry intend to resist the *presentation*, and have entered a caveat accordingly[2].'

Aware that a protest had been made to the Archbishop of York, Edward Venables-Vernon, Patrick respectfully declined his nomination, but fate took a hand. Reverend Heap repeated his mistake, and appointed Samuel Redhead to the Haworth curacy without consulting the villagers. Pandemonium reigned at Reverend Redhead's first two Sunday services, and the extreme and violent lengths the parishioners went to were attested to by Charles Longley, Bishop of Ripon and later Archbishop of Canterbury. He stayed at Haworth Parsonage on a pastoral visit in March 1853, and Patrick explained how he had come into the curacy there. It was a tale so fantastic that Bishop Longley immediately wrote to his wife Caroline with its details:

> 'There is an ancient feud between Bradford and Haworth ... the people of Haworth can by the trust deed of the living, prevent the person appointed by the vicar [of Bradford] from entering the Parsonage or receiving any of the emoluments, if he does not please them... in the case of Mr. Redhead, the inhabitants exercised their right of resistance and opposition and to such a point did they carry it, that they actually brought a Donkey into the church while Mr. Redhead was officiating and held up its head to stare him in the face – they then laid a plan to crush him to death in the vestry, by pushing a table against him as he was taking off his surplice and hanging it up, foiled in this for some reason or other they then turned out into the Churchyard where Mr. Redhead was going to perform a funeral and were determined to throw him into the grave and bury him alive[3].'

Reverend Redhead fled on horseback and escaped with his life. It was clear, however, that he could not return to Haworth at this juncture, and so at last Reverend Heap of Bradford met the villagers to find a compromise. The solution was that Patrick Brontë would after all become curate of Haworth, but it would be the parishioners who would nominate him.

Patrick and Maria moved to Haworth on 20 April 1820, and they both spent the rest of their lives there. There were ten in the party making the slow journey across the moors, for travelling alongside them were two servants, Nancy Garrs' younger sister Sarah having also been taken on as a further help, and their now six children. Their youngest child, another daughter, had been born just three months earlier and christened Anne after her maternal grandmother.

The letters sent to Elizabeth from Yorkshire seemed to bring good news upon good news, but at home in Penzance tragedy had struck again with the death of her only brother Benjamin, who failed suddenly in July 1818. Elizabeth not only had to attend the funeral of the brother she had taken such pride in, the man who had been known for his piety and business acumen alike, and who had brought honour to the Branwells by being made mayor of Penzance, she also had to watch his family fall apart.

Benjamin's wife Mary was not used to economising, and eventually had to place her property into the hands of her brother, as recalled in 1855, in a letter sent by Eliza Kingston, the niece of Elizabeth and Benjamin who had been brought to England as a baby, to her brother-in-law Joseph in America:

> 'My only Maternal Uncle Benjamin Branwell died when I was about 10 years old. He had the bulk of my Grandfather's property which he left, I understand, rather embarrassed to a widow and 7 children, 3 sons and 4 daughters. Mrs. Branwell and 2 of the sons have been dead some years. She was extravagant and wasted her property, the residue of which she sold to her brother, Mr. J. Batten, and he allowed her an annuity for herself and daughters, the greater part of which fell off at her death. The remainder, which is not quite £17 per year each, they still enjoy, and 3 of them keep a School. The fourth lives alone [Lydia], being in delicate health and rather peculiar in her ways[4].'

In early 1821, the letters Elizabeth received from her sister Maria came to a sudden halt, and the next letter she received from Yorkshire was in a less familiar hand. Ripping open the envelope, not standing on ceremony this time, she knew something was terribly wrong.

The letter[5] was from her brother-in-law Patrick, and although containing all the necessary formality it was obviously written under great strain. He related that Maria, without any prior warning whatsoever, had fallen gravely ill on 29 January 1821, and although she lingered on in great pain, and received all the medical attention available, it seemed that she would undoubtedly soon die. To add to Patrick's turmoil, his six children had all now contracted scarlet fever, and their lives hung in the balance too.

A letter sent later to his friend Reverend John Buckworth recalls this dread turn of events, and is likely to resemble the letter he sent at the time to Elizabeth:

> 'I was at Haworth, a stranger in a strange land. It was under these circumstances, after every earthly prop was removed, that I was called on to bear the weight of the greatest load of sorrows that ever pressed upon me. One day, I remember it well; it was a gloomy day, a day of clouds and darkness, three of my little children were taken ill of scarlet fever; and, the day after, the remaining three were in the same condition. Just at that time death seemed to have laid his hand on my dear wife in a manner which threatened her speedy dissolution. She was cold and silent and seemed hardly to notice what was passing around her[6].'

Elizabeth's mind raced as she slumped into a chair, letter clenched tightly in her hand. Her sister, nephew, and five nieces, including her goddaughter Elizabeth, could all be on the brink of death while she was helpless 400 miles away. What could she do? Her heart breaking, it was not within her to wait silently in Cornwall for the next letter which would be contained within a cold, black border. This life in Cornwall was one she had known and loved since she was a child, but what was it compared to the family she had grown so close to in Thornton? She knew that she could be sacrificing everything, but she did so readily. A letter was hastily written and despatched to Patrick, with the news that she would follow it. A response would not have found Elizabeth in Penzance, but there was no need for a response as Elizabeth's reaction was just what Patrick had expected and prayed for.

Saying goodbye to Charlotte and her family once more, and doubtless making a further call upon Jane and Eliza, Elizabeth explained that she planned to return after Maria's illness had reached its conclusion, good or bad. In her heart, however, she must have suspected that this might not be the case. It was a sombre farewell, and as her coach crossed into Devon, she took one last, lingering look backwards; she would never see Cornwall again.

Elizabeth arrived in Haworth in the summer of 1821, and found that it was very different to Thornton. It was at a much higher elevation, and the church of St Michael and All Angels, and the parsonage behind it, were at the top of a very steep hill then called Kirkgate, now known as Main Street to the throngs of tourists who walk up its incline every year. It was also apparent that Haworth was a more industrial location with mills in its valley, and smoke rising from a plethora of woolcombers' houses.

Reaching the parsonage, she saw that beyond it lay a great expanse of moorland with the purple heather then just coming into bloom, but it held no beauty for her. Dreadfully fatigued from the journey made in the height of summer, and from the stressful anticipation of what she was about to see, Elizabeth crossed a bare garden, climbed seven short stone steps and rapped with some trepidation upon the door.

The Patrick Brontë that opened the door to her was markedly different to the one she had left in Thornton five years earlier; the weary signs of grief were etched upon his face, but he bowed deeply and greeted her with warmth. Behind him were Nancy and Sarah Garrs, who she knew, and then the children were introduced to her. Elizabeth, to her great relief, found that during the course of her journey all six children had recovered from scarlet fever. Maria and Elizabeth were now girls aged 8 and 6, Charlotte was no longer a baby, although she was small for her 5 years, Branwell, just turned 4, looked on with a confident gaze, and a toddling Emily remained with shy suspicion in a corner. Anne, the baby of one year, was in her cot, but looking down at her for the first time Elizabeth was struck by the Branwell family likeness already evident in the child; it is a likeness that can be seen today by comparing pictures of Anne, her mother, and her grandfather Thomas.

Once the introductions had been made, and despite her increasing tiredness, Elizabeth asked to be shown to her sister who, from the lack of mourning clothes within the house, she knew was still living. Patrick ushered her into a darkened room, from which, as they entered, a nursemaid in her late-twenties, whom Patrick had recently hired, exited with a haughty air. The sight that greeted Elizabeth was shocking; her younger sister was terribly gaunt, and lying cold and silent as the letter had foretold. Elizabeth whispered Maria's name, and her sister's head turned towards her; a thin hand reached out and was grasped with tender affection. Patrick walked quietly from the room, leaving the sisters together with their great love and their sorrow.

For the next few days, Elizabeth supervised the actions of the maid, Martha Wright, and she was far from impressed by what she saw. After conferring with Patrick, something he would become used to over the next twenty years, it was agreed that Martha's services were no longer needed.

Whether the dismissal was fair or not we shall never know, but it was remembered and resented by Martha, and it was she who was the source of the unflattering stories about Patrick, and to a lesser extent Elizabeth, in Mrs. Gaskell's biography of Charlotte[7].

Elizabeth herself now took charge of her sister's care, and there could have been no more attentive nurse, but as the days and weeks passed Maria's already parlous condition deteriorated. The local physician, Dr Thomas Andrew, was consulted regularly[8], and no expense was spared in seeking help from doctors and surgeons further afield, but it was all in vain. Those who loved Maria now prayed, not for her recovery, but for her release from further torment.

It is commonly believed today that Maria Brontë died from cancer of the uterus, but this was disputed by the pre-eminent obstetrician and gynaecologist, Professor Philip Rhodes, who examined the known facts surrounding her death in 1972. He concluded that it was unlikely that Maria would have cancer of the uterus at her age, 38, and after having given birth successfully to six children. He instead believed that Maria died as a result of an infection contracted after Anne's birth the year before:

> 'All in all, I would lean to the idea of chronic pelvic sepsis together with increasing anaemia as the probable cause of her death. It is to be remembered that this was before the age of bacteriological knowledge ... Gynaecological knowledge was primitive, there was no ante-natal care and no attempt at follow-up after childbirth[9].'

Maria was often insensible or screaming in agony, but at times when the pain abated temporarily her focus was always on her children, although Martha Wright reported that sometimes she would only see one child at a time as otherwise it upset her too greatly as she thought of how they would soon be left motherless[10]. At other time she would call out 'Oh God - my poor children![11]'; it was almost too much for Elizabeth to bear but she sat by her sister's side through it all. Whether verbally or simply by a knowing smile, she let Maria know that she would be there for her children, come what may.

Elizabeth and Patrick were at the head of Maria's bedside on 15 September 1821, when she drew her last, strained breath and after eight months of agony achieved a final peace. Conventions put to one side, Patrick and Elizabeth placed their arms around each other and wept bitterly, as they embarked upon days of stunned, silent mourning. Patrick had lost the woman he loved, and without the presence of his sister-in-law it would have been beyond his endurance. He paid tribute to Elizabeth's role at this time in his letter to John Buckland two months after Maria's death:

'Her sister, Miss Branwell, arrived, and afforded great comfort to my mind, which has been the case ever since, by sharing my labours and sorrows, and behaving as an affectionate mother to my children[12].'

Elizabeth Branwell had done her duty, but neither she nor her brother-in-law could have known she would continue to do it for another twenty-one years.

Chapter 9

This May Be Her Home as Long as She Lives

"'My aunt is particularly fond of flowers," she observed, "and she is fond of Staningley too: I brought you here to offer a petition in her behalf that this may be her home as long as she lives, and – if it be not our home likewise – that I may often see her and be with her; for I fear she will be sorry to lose me; and, though she leads a retired and contemplative life, she is apt to get low-spirited if left too much alone."'

Anne Brontë, *The Tenant of Wildfell Hall*

Elizabeth probably planned to spend around a year in Haworth, as she had done in Thornton in happier times; this would give her time to observe a proper and correct mourning period for her sister Maria, and to ensure that a suitable maid was in place to look after her nephew and nieces; she even hoped that her brother-in-law would find another wife who could then become a second mother to the children, allowing her to return to Cornwall with a more optimistic heart. It was not to be.

Patrick had been very much in love with Maria, which wasn't necessarily to be expected at a time when many married for social or financial reasons. His wife's death left him bereft of energy, bereft of hope almost, but he knew that he must carry on for the sake of his children. It needed little prompting from Elizabeth for him to realise also that he should look for a second wife.

It was commonplace for widowers to re-marry quickly after the death of their spouse, especially if they had a young family. A perfect example of this was John Firth of Kipping House, who married Anne Greame just a year after his first wife Elizabeth was killed in a tragic accident after being thrown from a horse[1].

Patrick and John had been very close in Thornton, and he would have made an ideal confidante at this time of grieving, but unfortunately for Patrick, Dr Firth himself died at the end of 1820, and Patrick had returned to Thornton to conduct his funeral shortly before Maria fell mortally ill[2].

Despite having lost her father so recently, the 23-year-old Elizabeth Firth still went out of her way to help the Brontë family at their time of need. She visited Haworth Parsonage more than once during Maria's final illness, and on 26 May, she and her friend Fanny Outhwaite, who like Elizabeth had a year earlier been made a godmother to Anne Brontë, brought the eldest children, Maria and Elizabeth, to Kipping House for a month to offer them some respite[3].

As the sad year 1821 drew to a close, Patrick and Elizabeth Branwell shared not only fond reminiscences of Maria but also frank discussions about what they were to do next. Inevitably talks of another marriage often surfaced, but Patrick's ham-fisted attempts to secure a wife would prove highly ineffectual. One example came in 1823, when he wrote to a woman named Mary Burder in Wethersfield, Essex, who he had seemingly been engaged to at the start of his career as a minister. The reason for the breaking off of their engagement is not known, but it was clearly something Mary remembered with bitter clarity, as her reply to his postal proposal a decade-and-a-half later shows:

'Whether those ardent professions of devoted lasting attachment were sincere is now to me a matter of but little consequence. "What I have seen and heard" certainly leads me to conclude very differently. With these my present views of past occurrences is it possible think you that I or my dear Parent could give you a cordial welcome to the Park as an *old friend?* Indeed I must give a decided negative to the desired visit. I know of no ties of friendship *ever* existing between us which the last eleven or twelve years have not severed or at least placed an insuperable bar to any revival[4].'

Mary Burder was not the only name to be crossed off the list of potential suitors. In January 1824, we have a letter from Isabella Dury of Keighley, four miles from Haworth, to her friend Miss Mariner. Isabella was the younger sister of Reverend Theodore Dury, the vicar of Keighley and a friend of Patrick, but she seems to have taken his proposal less than seriously:

'I heard before I left Keighley that my brother & I had quarrelled about poor Mr Brontë, I beg you if ever you hear such a report that you will contradict it as I can assure you it is perfectly unfounded, I think I never should be so very silly as to have the most distant idea of marrying anybody who had not some fortune, and six children into the bargain. It is too ridiculous to imagine any truth in it[5].'

The first rejection Patrick had was a particularly crushing one as it came from a woman he held in the highest esteem; a woman that Elizabeth thought highly of too, the woman she had burst into tears at when taking her departure five years earlier – Elizabeth Firth.

Elizabeth Branwell encouraged Patrick to make the attempt. Here was a woman who already knew and loved the children, and was even godmother to two of them; she was kind and caring, as demonstrated by her actions during Maria's illness, and after the death of her father she was also a woman of some means. If Patrick could convince Miss Firth to become his wife, then Elizabeth would be free to return to Cornwall. It was a fervent hope, but she must have suspected all along that it was also a forlorn one.

Elizabeth Firth was shocked and dismayed at the proposal from the man who was twenty-one years her senior, and whose wife, who she had held as a great friend, had died only three months previously. Her diary entry for 14 December 1821 is twelve words long, eight of them underlined, but it conceals much:

'I wrote my last letter to Mr Brontë. Mr Franks to dinner[6].'

The letter formalised her rejection of Patrick's proposal of marriage. There is then a gap of fourteen days with no diary entries; presumably Elizabeth was too angry to lift her pen. This anger lasted two years, during which she had no communication at all with Patrick, although the healing properties of time, and her kindly nature, eventually led to them regaining friendly terms. The Mr Franks she referred to in her diary was Reverend James Franks, a man who held Elizabeth's heart and whom she later married.

These three brutal rejections, and there may have been more we don't know of, made it quite clear to both Patrick Brontë and Elizabeth Branwell by the start of 1824 that he would never find another wife; with a large family, little income and his advancing years, he was no longer husband material. Even a marriage of convenience between Patrick and his sister-in-law, which might otherwise have been considered for the sake of the children, was impossible because it was outlawed under incest laws.

There was now a big decision to be made by Elizabeth, one that would completely change the course of her life. As the wind howled under the parsonage door, as it was so apt to do, she thought of warmer evenings in joyous Penzance, and the sisters, nephews and nieces she'd left there. Candle fluttering, she walked quietly around the house, past the large grandfather clock that stood in the centre of the staircase, and looked in at the bedrooms where her sister's children were sleeping. Finally, she entered the room which had for over two-and-a-half years been her own. They were children she had come to love immensely, and there in a small bed in her room slept the quiet, gentle Anne; now just past her fourth birthday and with no memories of her mother, but a great need for one. Elizabeth blew out the candle, the decision was made.

After breakfast Elizabeth informed Patrick of her decision to remain at the parsonage until the children were married or in situations of their own. Patrick nodded his head in silent gratitude. He knew what a vast sacrifice his sister-in-law was making; after all, she had now willingly become, like the phrase used in his letter to John Buckworth, 'a stranger in a strange land'. No more would she see the rolling waves break upon the rocks of Mount Bay, the shanties and songs would fade from memory, and the year-round warmth of Penzance would be replaced by wet summers and harsh winters that brought colds, coughs and worse.

A letter was sent to Charlotte and Joseph informing them of her decision, and asking for items of her property to be sent on to Haworth. Thankfully, Elizabeth's goods avoided the shipwrecked fate of Maria's, and a selection of them can be seen at the Brontë Parsonage Museum. These items allow us an insight into Elizabeth Branwell's mind and life, and they include a white nightcap with intricate lace adornment, a beautiful smelling salts bottle with gold trimming, pictures of flowers and the initial EB on the back (Maria had a matching salts bottle with MB on the reverse, so perhaps they were a present from their parents), the lacquered dressing case that meant so much to her, and a pair of wood and iron pattens.

These pattens, designed for outside use, were worn by Elizabeth inside the parsonage as well, and are commented upon in two very different descriptions we have of her at this time. Firstly, we have Ellen Nussey's depiction:

'Miss Branwell was a very small, antiquated little lady. She wore caps large enough for half a dozen of the present fashion, and in front of light auburn curls over her forehead. She always dressed in silk. She had a horror of the climate so far north, and of the stone floors in the parsonage. She amused us by clicking about in pattens whenever she had to go into the kitchen or look after household operations[7].'

Ellen did concede, however, that Elizabeth 'probably had been pretty[8]' in her youth. We also get a rather more flattering description of Elizabeth's appearance and apparel from reports given to the early-twentieth century Brontë biographer, Ellis Chadwick, by elderly Haworth residents who still recalled the woman from Cornwall:

'Those who once remembered her told the writer that she was never to be seen without a shoulder shawl, and several of these shawls are still in existence. Shades of purple and mauve were her favourite colours. Her caps, if large, were always dainty, and her dresses good and becoming – a black silk being her favourite for afternoon wear. Fine dresses were not suitable for the stone floors and rough roads of Haworth, but in order to keep her dainty shoes dry and avoid the damp floors she was in the habit of wearing pattens, much to the annoyance of her nieces, whose sensitive nerves were irritated by the constant and peculiar click of the iron rings on the stone floors[9].'

Elizabeth's decision to remain in Haworth was a godsend to Patrick, not only for the assistance she would provide in raising his children, but also for the financial assistance that she contributed. Patrick Brontë earned around £170 per year as Haworth's priest, but the family income had been supplemented by Maria's £50 a year that she received from her father's will. With Maria's death, this vital addition was gone. The Haworth trustees were also able to withhold part of his wage, if they saw fit, and he also had to pay for any repairs carried out on church land. On 25 August 1825, after having to pay for a particularly expensive repair, he was forced to write to the Queen Anne's Bounty board, who supported impoverished clergymen, stating that his bills were:

'A very large amount, rendering the salary inadequate to support my family, even with the most rigorous economy[10].'

His request was declined at this time, and further economies had to be made, although he may also have received financial assistance from his friends, including Elizabeth. Patrick Brontë was a proud man, but had no option other than to be realistic, and he could ill-afford to turn down loans and gifts that were offered to him in times of need. Never was this needed more than after the death of Maria, as he had exhausted all his savings and run up considerable debts, in the search for a cure. The Morgans and Fennells, the Elizabeths Firth and Branwell, Reverends Buckworth and Redhead, who unlike Patrick, were clergymen from wealthy backgrounds, and others, cleared Patrick's debts that would otherwise have led to penury for him and his young family. He received £150 from his friends[11], and a banknote for the substantial amount of £50 from 'a benevolent individual, a wealthy lady, in the West Riding of Yorkshire[12]'. This woman is now believed to have been a wealthy estate owner from Eshton Hall in North Yorkshire who was noted for her works of charity and support of the clergy; her name would, by coincidence or otherwise, become associated with Patrick's third daughter: she was Miss Frances Richardson-Currer, a likely source of the pen-name Currer Bell later adopted by Charlotte Brontë

Elizabeth had quickly discerned the financial situation that the Brontës were in after her arrival in Haworth in the summer of 1821, and realised that it would become much worse after her sister's death. Approaching Patrick as tactfully as possible, she told him that one of the conditions of her staying at the parsonage was that she would pay rent out of the annuity she received, as if she wasn't allowed to do so it would be an affront to her pride[13]. In this way she replaced Maria's contribution with her own, although she still managed to keep some money in reserve to add to her established savings – money that would later be used to support her nieces in a variety of endeavours, even after her death.

An additional opportunity to be of financial assistance came in July 1824, when Maria and Elizabeth were sent to the Clergy Daughters' School at Cowan Bridge in what is now Cumbria. Charlotte followed in August, and Emily arrived at the end of the year. We have a letter that Patrick addressed to his bank manager on 10 November 1824 in anticipation of Emily's departure:

'Dear Sir, I take this opportunity to give you notice that in the course of a fortnight it is my intention to draw about twenty pounds out of your savings bank. I am going to send another of my little girls to school, which at the first will cost me some little – but in the end I shall not lose[14].'

We will see just how much he was about to lose at the school famously, and infamously, portrayed as Lowood in *Jane Eyre*, but he and Elizabeth would have felt no forebodings at the time. Maria and Elizabeth Brontë had already enjoyed a term at Crofton Hall school near Wakefield, an establishment with an excellent reputation and one that had been attended by Brontë godmothers, Elizabeth Firth and Fanny Outhwaite, who probably paid most of the fees on this occasion. Nevertheless, it was an expensive school to attend, and Patrick couldn't expect the women to pay the Crofton Hall fees interminably, so he looked for a more affordable option.

Elizabeth's opinion was sought on the school he found; it was newly-established but as it was designed purposely for daughters of the clergy, and run by a clergyman himself, Reverend Carus Wilson, Elizabeth had no reason to doubt that it would prove eminently suitable. Up to this point, she had been teaching the children herself, but she knew that a formal education would help her nieces secure jobs in the future, and it is likely that she also helped to pay the school fees. Standing outside the parsonage, waving at the carriage that drove Maria and Elizabeth away from her, she felt the swelling of pride and sorrow so familiar to parents today as they watch their child leave for their first day at school.

Patrick, who travelled with his children on this occasion, would greatly miss the company of his eldest daughter Maria, who was already showing prodigious gifts and with whom he could converse on any subject of the day as if she was an adult. Elizabeth, on the other hand, was more saddened at the departure of her niece of the same name, a girl she had formed a strong attraction to since being named as her godmother. The then eight-year-old Elizabeth's academic achievements were assessed by the school upon her entry:

> 'Reads little. Writes pretty well. Ciphers none. Works very badly. Knows nothing of grammar, history, geography or accomplishments[15].'

We should not read too much into this report as most of the pupils, including Maria and Charlotte, had similarly critical appraisals, although the young Emily garnered an unusually glowing report. What is telling, however, is that the school records also show what profession the girls are to be schooled for. Maria, Charlotte and Emily are listed as future governesses, while Elizabeth is listed as being prepared for the role of a housekeeper.

Elizabeth may not have been as academically gifted as her sisters, but she was a kind and practical girl, and these qualities are sure to have won the affection of her aunt. She was also stoic in the face of pain, as remembered by the Superintendent of the school, Miss Evans:

> 'The second, Elizabeth, is the only one of the [Brontë] family of whom I have a vivid recollection, from her meeting with a rather alarming accident, in consequence of which I had her for some days and nights in my bed-room, not only for the sake of her greater quiet, but that I might watch over her myself. Her head was severely cut, but she bore all the consequent suffering with exemplary patience, and by it won much upon my esteem[16].'

It is clear that Elizabeth had suffered a terrible injury, but far worse was to come for her and her sister Maria. The story has often been told, not least in a disguised form in *Jane Eyre*, of how the atrocious conditions of Cowan Bridge, its poor food, strict discipline and unhealthy location, 'transformed the seminary into a hospital[17]'. Epidemics of typhoid and tuberculosis broke out, and Maria was among the first to succumb; she was sent home to Haworth suffering from 'ill health' as the school recorded it, with Elizabeth also returned just a month later. They died of tuberculosis with their father and aunt watching over them on 6 May and 15 June 1825 respectively, at just 11 and 10 years old.

It was a devastating occurrence for Elizabeth Branwell, who had encouraged the children to be sent to the school, and helped to pay for it. She had left the warmth and light of Penzance for this, a windswept house where she had already witnessed three people die; the little girl she had held in her arms at Thornton's church ten years earlier, making solemn vows before God to protect her, was now held lifeless in those same arms. Patrick, consumed by grief and anger, fetched Charlotte and Emily home forthwith; unable to bear the loss of another child they would now be taught at home, and Elizabeth Branwell, veteran of the penny school on Chapel Street, was given the central role.

Chapter 10

Curiosity and a Quick Intellect

'He took her education entirely on himself, and made it an amusement. Fortunately, curiosity and a quick intellect made her an apt scholar: she learned rapidly and eagerly, and did honour to his teaching.'

Emily Brontë, *Wuthering Heights*

As a child, Elizabeth Branwell had learned largely from her parents, although external tutors may also have been used. Years later she put those lessons to good use as she passed on all she knew to the Brontë children. They were, in general, able and eager students, although they also demonstrated a mischievous streak from time to time.

After the return of Charlotte and Emily from Cowan Bridge, the children's education became the responsibility of Elizabeth and her brother-in-law. Patrick took upon himself primarily the teaching of Branwell, leaving his three girls to take instruction from their aunt. As is evident from their novels, the Brontë sisters were highly intelligent women with a wide breadth of knowledge, even though the lessons given by their Aunt Branwell were not always to their taste.

Elizabeth had no doubt how prodigious her nieces were, even from the youngest age, but she also knew that their cleverness and talent would be of little use to them in later life unless it was channelled correctly. For that reason, practical subjects were always at the heart of her schooling, and she drummed into Charlotte, Emily and Anne by repetition, the skills that would be most helpful in obtaining a post of governess or teacher. Among these skills were reading and arithmetic, study of the Bible, and a smattering of history and geography.

These lessons were carried out in the bedroom that Elizabeth shared with her youngest niece Anne, with the beds pushed back to create space for the classroom. Above all else, they were taught sewing[1], spending hours working upon making clothing or repairing it. This was especially trying to

Charlotte, who had inherited her father's poor eyesight, and for whom the intricate skills of needlework were a severe physical test as well as a test of patience. The girls had little option but to submit to Elizabeth's directions, tiresome though they found it, as their aunt knew this was a skill vital for both today and tomorrow.

The Brontë children could not afford to buy new clothing at regular intervals as many others of their social standing did, so they had to rely on hand-me-downs, in the case of the younger children Emily or Anne, or repair their clothes until they could be repaired no more. This had the inevitable effect of leaving their clothing behind the times, something that was also levelled at Elizabeth Branwell herself in a letter sent by Charlotte's friend Mary Taylor to Elizabeth Gaskell after the publication of her biography of Charlotte Brontë:

> 'When I saw Miss Branwell she was a very precise person, and looked very odd, because her dress was so utterly out of fashion. She corrected one of us once for using the word "spit" or "spitting." She made a great favourite out of Branwell. She made her nieces sew, with purpose or without, and as far as possible discouraged any other culture. She used to keep the girls sewing charity clothing, and maintained to me that it was not for the good of the recipients but of the sewers[2].'

Mary Taylor was herself a very precise and forthright person, but although she shared a school, Roe Head in Mirfield, with Charlotte, she came from a much wealthier family, and does Elizabeth a great disservice in her description above. Mary Taylor saw her on only a few brief visits, and could not have known Elizabeth's own background, nor that she had loved fashion in her own younger days but was now putting aside her own desires in order to save money for her nephew and nieces. This was an act of charity akin to the charity work she made her charges do, but she was confident that these acts of kindness were themselves an essential lesson that would bring their own reward.

Charlotte herself later found how useful her needlework classes had been when she took on a short-lived job as governess to the White family of Rawdon:

> 'Mrs White expects a good deal of sewing from me – I cannot sew "much" during the day on account of the children – who require the closest attention[3].

Elizabeth also took it upon herself to instruct the children in cooking and how to keep a home, lessons that she knew her sister Maria would have provided. Under her instruction, and her supervision of the parsonage servants Nancy and Sarah Garrs and later Tabby Aykroyd, the parsonage was kept spotlessly clean, a thing often commented upon by visitors.

Nevertheless, children will be children, and the Brontës would on occasion talk back to their aunt, or complain that they would rather be out playing, as we see in Emily and Anne's diary paper of 24 November 1834. Emily and Anne produced regular diary papers at three or four yearly intervals. This first extant diary paper was written jointly by the sisters who were so close to each other that they were described by Ellen Nussey as being like twins in all but appearance[4], arms constantly entwined. By this time, they were 16 and 14 respectively, but still being instructed by their aunt and being watched over by her eagle eye:

> 'Aunt has just come into the kitchen now and said where are your feet Anne, Anne answered on the floor Aunt ... It is past Twelve o'clock, Anne and I have not tidied ourselves, done our bed work or done our lessons and we want to go out to play[5].'

It seems that Elizabeth had walked into the kitchen and found Anne swinging her legs through the air, or perhaps leaning back dangerously in her chair, and even though she had developed a great affection for her youngest niece, she was not going to let this go without admonishment. Without doubt the girls would also have had to finish their lessons before going out to play, just as later in the diary paper Emily has to lay down her pen and help Tabby with the task of peeling potatoes.

Tabby Aykroyd arrived as a servant at Haworth Parsonage in 1824, after Nancy Garrs had left to be married, with her sister Sarah leaving shortly after. Tabby was then 53, five years older than Elizabeth, and remained at the parsonage until her death in 1855, except for a period of around three years that she spent with her sister Susannah while she recovered from a serious leg injury[6].

Patrick stated that he decided to employ Tabby because he thought that one 'elderly' woman would be better for his children than two young ones[7]. This decision was reached after consultation with Elizabeth, who now shared with him in all major household decisions. Called in to the parsonage for an informal interview, Elizabeth was impressed by the straight-talking Yorkshire woman's common sense approach as well as by the practical skills she possessed. It also meant that Elizabeth would no longer be the oldest person in the parsonage, which, although she was never a vain woman, was no doubt a relief.

Elizabeth and Patrick had made a fortuitous decision, for Tabby became far more than just a servant within the household, she was also a friend to the children and much loved by them. This affection was forged during her early years at the parsonage, when as she was cleaning floors or baking bread she would relate stories of local folklore and legend. It is commonly accepted that these stories had an influence on the girls, an influence that is most apparent in the gothic tones of Wuthering Heights. Undoubtedly, Tabby's tales were one step along the road to the Brontë novels we love today, but just as important and just as evident are the stories told them by their Aunt Branwell.

Elizabeth's idle hours were often spent in solitary reflection upon the life she had known in Penzance, but she was also a loquacious woman who would talk about it whenever she had a willing audience, and to her delight she found that her nephew and nieces were always ready to listen to a good story, even if it was one she may have told once or twice before. This trait was so central to Elizabeth's character that Ellen Nussey could not help but notice it whenever she visited the parsonage, but she talked not only of the balls and 'gaities of her dear native town[8]', but also of the strange stories and legends that she had grown up with, some of which were very close to home.

A building near to the one Elizabeth had grown up in on Chapel Street was widely reputed to be haunted by the ghost of its previous inhabitant Mrs Baines. The widow of a Captain Baines, she occupied a large house at 20, Chapel Street with an even larger orchard, and she was particularly proud of the apples that grew there. Mrs Baines was also aware that local children often stole into her orchard and crept away with armfuls of apples, and for this reason she set her servant John as a night watchman. Armed with a blunderbuss he sat in hiding within the orchard waiting for apple thieves to arrive. Given that he was charged to wait there all through the night it is little wonder that he sometimes fell asleep. Catching him dozing one night in 1803, Mrs Baines shook some apples from a tree to confront her guard with in the morning, but the rustling sound awoke John who, half-asleep, shot his mistress from close range.

Mrs Baines never recovered from her injuries, and the shocking story is sure to have been discussed within the neighbouring home of the Branwell family. Soon, however, a different kind of story began to circulate. It was said that the ghostly figure of an old woman now walked the Chapel Street orchard at night. Writing in the mid-nineteenth century, local historian William Bottrell recounted her fate:

'The ghost of Mrs. Baines was often seen under the tree where she was shot, or walking the rounds of her garden. Everybody knew the old lady by her upturned and powdered grey hair under a lace cap of antique pattern; by the long lace ruffles hanging from her elbows; her short silk mantle, gold-headed cane, and other trappings of old-fashioned pomp... Sometimes she would flutter up from the garden or yard (just like an old hen flying before the wind), and perch herself on the wall[9].'

Bottrell then recounts how eventually a priest had to exorcise the ghost by chasing her to the Penzance beach, and binding her to spin ropes of sand for a thousand years. It is a fantastical tale based upon a real life tragedy, and one the Brontë children would have loved to hear, especially when Elizabeth explained how she and their mother had often walked past the orchard, hand in hand and afraid to cast a backward glance.

A ghost story involving their own family was a sheer thrill to the children, and it remained fresh in Charlotte's memory at the time she placed a ghostly nun into her novel *Villette*:

'Yes; there scarce stirred a breeze, and that heavy tree was convulsed, while the feathery shrubs stood still... With a sort of angry rush – close, close past our faces – swept swiftly the very NUN herself! Never had I seen her so clearly. She looked tall of stature, and fierce of gesture. As she went, the wind rose sobbing; the rain poured wild and cold; the whole night seemed to feel her[10].'

Mrs Baines wasn't the only ghostly presence associated with Chapel Street at the time Elizabeth Branwell lived there. A ghostly figure clad in white was often seen in the graveyard of St Mary's church[11]. Locals often refused to walk past it at night, but as it was just a few steps from Elizabeth's house she would have had little choice but to.

There was one further graveyard story the young Brontës heard; a tragic event etched in Elizabeth's mind. Philippa Tyack, the wife of Robert Matthews Branwell, died on 28 August 1818. It is said that at

Philippa's funeral her husband was so overcome with grief that he threw himself on top of the coffin as it was being covered with soil, and then scraped the soil away crying out her name inconsolably[12]. As Elizabeth was at that time living with Joseph and Charlotte, the deceased's brother-in-law and sister-in-law, it seems most likely that she would have been at the funeral to witness this terrible outpouring of grief.

The story of a wild man tearing away soil from a coffin is familiar to us today, not from the true story of Robert Matthews Branwell but from one of the greatest fictional stories of all time, set down on paper by his first cousin once removed, Emily Brontë:

> 'It scraped the coffin; I fell to work with my hands; the wood commenced cracking about the screws; I was on the point of attaining my object, when it seemed that I heard a sigh from some one above, close at the edge of the grave, and bending down. "If I can only get this off," I muttered, "I wish they may shovel in the earth over us both!"[13]'

Wuthering Heights is an almost unparalleled work of genius, and yet there are many clear influences upon it, from James Hogg's *The Private Memoirs and Confessions of a Justified Sinner* to Walter Scott's *The Bride of Lammermoor*, but we should not underestimate the importance of the tales she first heard at her aunt's knee. Walter Scott's influence can also be felt in Emily's prose and poetry, and he was hero-worshipped by Charlotte Brontë who wrote:

> 'For Fiction - read Scott alone, all novels after his are worthless.[14]'

Brontë lovers have a lot to be thankful for to the Edinburgh poet and novelist, and the Brontës in turn were thankful to Aunt Elizabeth, for it was she who first introduced them to his work in 1828. At Christmas of that year, she presented her nephew and nieces with a new work by Scott entitled *Tales of a Grandfather* and this thoughtful act would go on to have a huge impact on the history of literature.

Tales of a Grandfather is a selection of stories relating events from Scottish history from the time of Macbeth onwards, and its tales of adventure and intrigue set among the Scottish highlands and moorlands gripped the children's imagination from the first page; soon they were recreating scenes from the book on their daily walks, with the purple heather-clad moors of Haworth substituting for similar landscapes north of the border. This, along with Patrick's gift of a set of twelve wooden soldiers to his children in June 1826, proved a catalyst for the famous little books that the children made, based upon the imaginary lands of Angria, created by Charlotte and Branwell, and Gondal, created later by Emily and Anne.

They may have lacked the formal education many of their peers enjoyed, but they more than made up for this by the access to their father's library. Patrick had an extensive collection of books and he let his children, son and daughters alike, have free access to it. Many parents of this time would have found it scandalous that young girls were allowed to see works by the likes of Byron and the atheist Percy Shelley, but Patrick had more enlightened views and believed greatly in the power of education for both boys and girls, and that books should not be restricted to one sex rather than another. This opinion is also espoused by Anne Brontë in her preface to the second edition of *The Tenant of Wildfell Hall* in which she hits back at her critics:

> 'In my own mind, I am satisfied that if a book is a good one, it is so whatever the sex of the author may be. All novels are or should be written for both men and women to read, and I am at a loss to conceive how a man should permit himself to write anything that should be really disgraceful for a woman, or why a woman should be censured for writing anything that would be proper and becoming for a man[15].'

Just as important as Patrick's laissez-faire attitude when it came to reading matter is that it was wholeheartedly endorsed by Elizabeth. Remembering the joy that she had taken in reading books given to her by her parents or borrowed from the Penzance Ladies Library, she also did all she could to inculcate a love of reading in her nephew and nieces. It was this that lay behind Elizabeth's decision in 1832 to start a subscription to *Fraser's Magazine for Town and Country*. The magazine commented upon the political issues of the day, but it also contained reviews of the latest books, poetry and extracts from novels. It was also *Fraser's Magazine* that published two poems by Anne Brontë, 'The Three Guides' and 'The Narrow Way', making her the only sister who had her poetry printed without having to pay for it.

When Elizabeth informed her nieces of her new subscription they were delighted, although Charlotte's announcement of it in a letter to her brother is characteristically muted:

> 'I am extremely glad that Aunt has consented to take in *Fraser's Magazine* for though I know from a description of its general contents that it will be rather uninteresting when compared with "Blackwood" [*Blackwood's* was a similar magazine the Brontës especially loved as it was printed in Edinburgh] still it would be better than remaining the whole year without sight of any periodical publication whatever, and such would assuredly be our case as in the little wild, moorside village where we reside there would be no possibility of borrowing, or obtaining a work of that description from a circulating library[16].'

The books she bought and the magazines she subscribed to were just some of the many financial commitments she made on behalf of her sister's children, commitments that kept her in the same old-fashioned clothing year after year. Seeing her nieces reading, and later writing, together, however, made these sacrifices worthwhile. Elizabeth found that raising a family brought rewards she had never dreamed of in Penzance, and there was nothing she liked more than to see smiles play across the faces of her nieces; especially when such a smile spread across the face of the girl she had grown to love more than any other; Anne.

Chapter 11

My Kind, Prim Aunt

'At last, to my great joy, it was decreed that I should take charge of the young family of a certain Mrs Bloomfield; whom my kind, prim aunt Grey had known in her youth, and asserted to be a very nice woman.'

Anne Brontë, *Agnes Grey*

Charlotte Brontë's great friend, Ellen Nussey, first visited Haworth Parsonage in the summer of 1833, and her recollection of this visit is fascinating in many ways, detailing among other things how the garden was bare except for a few currant bushes, and how clean the house was as the hallway and stairs had been cleaned with sand stone[1] (in true Penzance fashion). Ellen also gave a description of Anne Brontë, then aged 13, that is particularly revealing about her relationship with her Aunt Branwell:

'Anne, dear, gentle Anne, was quite different in appearance from the others. She was her aunt's favourite. Her hair was a very pretty, light brown, and fell on her neck in graceful curls. She had lovely violet-blue eyes, fine pencilled eyebrows, and clear, almost transparent complexion[2].'

There are a number of reasons why Anne may have been the favourite of Elizabeth's nieces, and Ellen has touched upon one in her description of the youngest Brontë – she didn't look like her dark eyed, heavy featured sisters, but had instead inherited the Branwell traits of her mother. There is a noticeable similarity between portraits of Anne and her mother Maria, and with her grandfather Thomas Branwell, so this must have been even more evident to Elizabeth. As she watched Anne grow up, she was reminded more and more of her loved and lost sister Maria, and this is sure to have strengthened Elizabeth's feelings for her, as would the fact that she had the same name her mother had borne.

Elizabeth's protective nature was also stirred by Anne's frailty as a child, and into adulthood. Anne suffered from asthma, and the cold and blustery conditions of Haworth often brought on a wheezing, gasping attack. Without today's medication to control or prevent such attacks, they must have been terrifying both for Anne and for those who had to witness them, as we can see from Charlotte's description of one particularly savage bout of asthma:

> 'She [Anne] had two nights last week when her cough and difficulty of breathing were painful indeed to hear and witness, and must have been most distressing to suffer; she bore it, as she does all affliction, without one complaint, only sighing now and then when nearly worn out[3].'

Elizabeth witnessed many such attacks, and was often the first to comfort her niece during them, as for much of Anne's life she shared a room with her aunt[4], and in her childhood they shared the same bed. Such arrangements were common for the time, and a necessary expediency in the parsonage that at times housed up to ten people. A similar arrangement existed with Emily and Charlotte who also shared a room throughout their childhood and youth.

For Charlotte and Emily this was a particularly welcome arrangement, as it allowed them to continue to invent and act out stories, whispered from one sister to another, long after the candles had been snuffed. Charlotte wrote of these night time adventures in her 'History of the Year' of 1829:

> 'Our plays were established: Young Men, June 1826; Our Fellows, July 1827; Islanders, December 1827. These are our three great plays that are not kept secret. Emily's and my bed plays were established the 1st December 1827, the others March 1828. Bed plays mean secret plays. They are very nice ones. All our plays are very strange ones. Their nature I need not write on paper for I think I shall always remember them[5].'

Anne's evenings were very different of course, as there was no playing or story telling after the light went out in the room she shared with her aunt. That is not to say, however, that Elizabeth tried to stifle Anne's creativity; on the contrary, she was delighted to see and hear the stories her nephew and nieces were creating, as we can tell from the books that she bought them, and from her encouragement of their reading.

Sharing a room brought aunt and niece ever closer to each other, and a life-long love grew between them. Anne gives a hint of this in her first novel *Agnes Grey*. It is a great, if underrated, work of fiction, but it is largely autobiographical, dealing as it does with a young northern woman, the daughter of a clergyman, and her two positions as a governess. The novel mentions a kind and prim Aunt Grey, but we can also take the references within the novel to 'mother' to relate to Elizabeth Branwell also, as Anne had no memories of her actual mother Maria. One passage in the book reveals the closeness in childhood of Agnes and her mother, for which we should read Anne and Elizabeth:

> 'In my childhood I could not imagine a more afflictive punishment than for my mother to refuse to kiss me at night: the very idea was terrible. More than the idea I never felt, for, happily, I never committed a fault that was deemed worthy of such penalty; but once I remember, for some transgression of my sister's, our mother thought proper to inflict it upon her: what she felt, I cannot tell; but my sympathetic tears and suffering for her sake I shall not soon forget[5].'

This then is how Anne's childhood evenings were spent; she would retire to bed, say a prayer alongside her Aunt Elizabeth, wait for a kiss on the forehead, after which the candles would be blown out and they would settle down together to sleep. In this way Anne received the love and warmth from her aunt that cruel fate had denied her from her mother.

Whether by nature, or because of this nurture, Anne grew up to be highly religious like her aunt, although we shall see how her deep study of religion led to a physical and mental breakdown. One of Elizabeth's treasured possessions bought during her years at Haworth was a brown glazed teapot. One side of the teapot contains a large lettered quotation reading, 'To Me to live is Christ, To die is Gain', and on the reverse side is the name of the man who said it: 'Wm. Grimshaw, Haworth[6].'

William Grimshaw was a famous eighteenth century Wesleyan preacher, who had been one of Patrick Brontë's predecessors as Haworth's parson from 1742 to his death in 1763, and a man renowned for his sincerity and zeal, as well as for the extreme length of his sermons. During one Sunday morning service he fainted, but revived enough to tell the parishioners to wait in the church until he returned. He was carried to his house, and when he came round his first words were 'I have had a glorious vision from the third heaven[7]', after which he went back to the church and preached until seven in the evening.

Another story relating to Grimshaw's time in Haworth was that he sometimes asked for a long psalm to be read; during the reading he walked into the public houses surrounding St Michael and All Angels' church carrying a horse whip, and flogged the people within into the church. His piety could not be questioned, even if the renowned poet Robert Southey doubted the state of Grimshaw's mental health:

> 'In his unconverted state this person was certainly insane; and, had he given utterance at that time to the monstrous and horrible imaginations which he afterwards revealed to his spiritual friends, he would deservedly have been sent to Bedlam[8].'

Despite his horsewhipping of loiterers, his interminable sermons, and his talk of visions, or possibly because of them, William Grimshaw became immensely popular in Haworth, and on occasion held services out on the moors as the crowds were too big to fit into his church. Grimshaw's fame had reached Cornwall, and as the purchase of the teapot shows, one of the things that brightened Elizabeth's time in Haworth was the thought that she was living next to, and worshipping in, William Grimshaw's church.

Elizabeth Branwell was a devout woman who believed in the importance of studying the Bible, and she was not afraid of debating matters of politics and religion with her esteemed brother-in-law, as Ellen Nussey recalled:

> 'In summer she [Elizabeth] spent part of the afternoon in reading aloud to Mr Brontë. In the winter evenings she must have enjoyed this; for she and Mr Brontë had often to finish their discussions on what she had read when we all met for tea. She would be very lively and intelligent, and tilt arguments against Mr Brontë without fear[9].'

This is an illuminating and touching scene; we see Elizabeth's intelligence and her forthright spirit, but we also see her characteristic kindness. Patrick Brontë suffered from cataracts and, although he later had them cut away without anaesthetic, in his advancing years he was partially blind. Even in his late middle age, as here, Patrick's eyesight was so poor that he

MR. THOMAS BRANWELL

MERCHANT OF PENZANCE, FATHER OF MRS BRONTË AND GRANDFATHER OF CHARLOTTE BRONTË. HE DIED AT PENZANCE IN 1808.
PAINTED IN 1799   AGED 53.

ANN BRANWELL

(NEE CARNE) WIFE OF MR THOMAS BRANWELL, MERCHANT OF PENZANCE; MOTHER OF MRS BRONTË AND GRANDMOTHER OF CHARLOTTE BRONTË. SHE DIED AT PENZANCE IN 1808.
PAINTED IN 1799.   AGED 55.

ELIZABETH BRANWELL

DAUGHTER OF THOMAS BRANWELL, ELDER SISTER OF MRS BRONTË. THE AUNT WHO TOOK CHARGE OF THE YOUNG BRONTËS AFTER THE DEATH OF THEIR MOTHER (HER SISTER). BORN 1776.   DIED 1841.
PAINTED IN 1799.

MARIA BRANWELL

DAUGHTER OF THOMAS AND ANN BRANWELL OF PENZANCE AND MOTHER OF CHARLOTTE BRONTË. MARRIED THE REV. P. BRONTË AT GUISELEY, YORKS. DECEMBER 29TH 1812.
BORN 1783.   DIED 1821.
PAINTED BY MR TARLIN AT PENZANCE IN THE YEAR 1799.

LIEUT. THOMAS BRANWELL R.N.

LOST IN THE FOUNDERING OF THE ST GEORGE IN THE BALTIC. BROTHER OF JOSEPH BRANWELL WHO MARRIED CHARLOTTE BRANWELL, HIS FIRST COUSIN AND YOUNGEST SISTER OF MRS BRONTË.

CHARLOTTE BRANWELL

YOUNGEST SISTER OF MRS BRONTË AND DAUGHTER OF THOMAS AND ANN BRANWELL. SHE MARRIED HER COUSIN JOSEPH BRANWELL DEC. 29TH 1812. BORN 1790.
PAINTED IN 1799.   AGED 9.

CHARLOTTE BRANWELL

DAUGHTER OF THOMAS AND ANN BRANWELL OF PENZANCE AND YOUNGEST SISTER OF MRS BRONTË. SHE MARRIED HER COUSIN JOSEPH BRANWELL DECEMBER 29TH 1812. PAINTED 1837.   AGED 47. GRANDMOTHER OF CAPTAIN AND MRS A. BRANWELL.

JOSEPH BRANWELL

OF PENZANCE MARRIED HIS COUSIN CHARLOTTE BRANWELL WHO WAS THE SISTER OF MRS BRONTË, DECEMBER 29TH 1812. GRANDFATHER OF CAPT. AND MRS A. BRANWELL.

ANN KINGSTON

ELDEST SISTER OF MRS BRONTË AND DAUGHTER OF THOMAS AND ANN BRANWELL.

PAINTED IN 1799.

SARAH HANNAH BRANWELL

WIFE OF THOMAS BRONTE BRANWELL (WHO WAS FIRST COUSIN OF CHARLOTTE BRONTË).

MR THOMAS BRONTE BRANWELL

BORN 1814   DIED 1897.

NEPHEW OF MR BRONTË.

CHARLES HENRY BRANWELL

SON OF JOSEPH BRANWELL (FIRST COUSIN OF MRS BRONTË) AND CHARLOTTE BRANWELL (YOUNGEST SISTER OF MRS BRONTË)

CAPT. ARTHUR BRANWELL

FIRST COUSIN OF CHARLOTTE BRONTË BRANWELL GRANDSON OF CHARLOTTE BRANWELL (YOUNGEST SISTER OF MRS BRONTË) AND HER FIRST COUSIN JOSEPH BRANWELL.

MRS CHARLOTTE BRONTE BRANWELL

COUSIN AND WIFE OF CAPTAIN A. BRANWELL (GRANDSON OF CHARLOTTE AND JOSEPH BRANWELL)

The Branwell family miniature portraits (courtesy of the Brontë Society)

View of Penzance from Lescudjack, early nineteenth century

(*Above left*) Silhouette of Elizabeth Branwell (courtesy of the Brontë Society)

(*Above right*) Elizabeth Branwell by James Tonkin, 1799 (courtesy of the Brontë Society)

(*Above left*) 'The Brontë Sisters' (l to r: Anne, Emily, Charlotte) by Patrick Branwell Brontë, c. 1835 (© National Portrait Gallery, London)

(*Above right*) Charlotte Brontë by George Richmond, 1850 (© National Portrait Gallery, London)

St. Michael's Mount by James Webb

Acton Castle, seen from Chapel Street, Penzance

Haworth Parsonage (© Janet Brown)

Aunt Branwell display, Brontë Parsonage Museum (© Brontë Parsonage Museum)

The Branwell house at 25 Chapel Street, Penzance

(*Above left*) Silhouette of Joseph Branwell (© Sarah Mason Walden)

(*Above right*) View of Coffin End from Elizabeth Branwell's room, Thornton Parsonage (© Mark de Luca)

View of Baltimore by William H. Bartlett, early 19th century

Thomas Brontë Branwell and
Charlotte Branwell, cousins of the
Brontë sisters (© Penlee House,
Penzance)

Chapel Street Wesleyan church, Penzance

found it hard to read, but without being asked, Elizabeth made it her daily task to read to him and bring some light into his darkening world.

Her theological debates with Patrick were mirrored in the discussions she had with Anne, and she was delighted to find that from an early age her youngest niece shared her enthusiasm for the scriptures and for debating their finer points. These were regular conversations in their shared room, but Anne later committed an example of them to paper in a little-known article hidden away in the archives of the Brotherton Library in Leeds.

Amidst their collection is a manuscript notebook in which Arthur Bell Nicholls, Charlotte's widower, wrote out by hand some of his late wife's poetry that had remained unpublished. The book he used must have been one that had been in Charlotte's possession, for the first eleven pages contain an unfinished dialogue between two people named simply C and S. Arthur has then turned the book around and started from what would have been the back of the book, so that his transcription of Charlotte's poems has the reverse orientation to this original work.

The handwriting shows without a doubt that the unfinished dialogue is by Anne Brontë[10], and it is a philosophical and theological discussion between C, who believes in the Bible, and S, who doesn't. We can guess that C & S represent Christ and Satan, although they seem to be on friendly terms with each other, but the atheistic character of S may also represent Emily Brontë as the C character says:

> 'Intimate as we have been from our childhood, we have always
> been strangely reserved upon the subject of religion[11].'

The opening of this piece is especially interesting as S berates C for still believing in the doctrines drummed into him by his nurse and mother:

> 'My dear C – it is most surprising that a man of your information
> and discernment should not yet have cast aside the prejudices
> instilled into him by his nurse and mother.'
> 'And is it because your mother has taught you to believe in the
> Bible, that you now refuse to credit it?'
> 'Not precisely; but because my mother taught me this doctrine
> I was doubly anxious to examine it for myself[12].'

Once again, Anne is walking upon autobiographical ground, and as in *Agnes Grey* the word 'mother' is used as a reference to her aunt. From it we see how Anne welcomed the Bible studies and doctrinal debates with Elizabeth, whereas their shared beliefs were soon abandoned by Emily.

Anne became an enthusiastic Biblical scholar, even studying it in its original Greek to ensure that it had been translated correctly, and this allowed her as an adult to tilt arguments against Elizabeth without fear, just as her aunt did against her father, and just as Helen does against her aunt in *The Tenant of Wildfell Hall*:

> 'Oh, Helen! Where did you learn all this?'
> 'In the Bible, aunt. I have searched it through, and found nearly thirty passages, all tending to support the same theory[13].'

Elizabeth's influence on Anne's education and character could be seen in more than just her love of the Bible; it was also evident in the kind, gentle nature that she became famous for, and her belief in the importance of family. Whereas Elizabeth showed this by moving to Haworth to raise her sister's children, Anne demonstrated it by such actions as finding her brother Branwell a job when it seemed he had little hope of finding one.

The love that Elizabeth had held for the infant Anne never diminished, and indeed it strengthened as she saw the fine woman she was becoming. It was with something approaching maternal pride that Elizabeth unrolled a certificate Anne placed into her hands in December 1836. It read:

> 'A prize for good conduct presented to Miss A. Brontë with Miss Wooler's kind love, Roe Head, Dec. 14th 1836.'

Miss Margaret Wooler was headmistress at Roe Head School at Mirfield, a town 18 miles south-west of Haworth. In January 1831, Charlotte was sent to Roe Head for her first formal schooling in five-and-a-half years. Elizabeth and Patrick had decided that whilst the children had made good progress under their joint tutelage, a more formal education would help them polish the accomplishments they would need to work as a governess.

Roe Head was a very different school to Cowan Bridge, and the enlightened Miss Wooler provided a safe and happy environment for her pupils to grow. It was here that Charlotte made her lifelong friends Ellen Nussey and Mary Taylor, both of whom would come to know Elizabeth Branwell, Ellen on friendly terms but Mary rather less so.

After just over a year at Roe Head, Charlotte returned to Haworth and she was then charged with the task of teaching her younger sisters what she had learned at the school. In July 1835, however, Charlotte returned to Roe Head, this time in the capacity of teacher. The salary was low, but the terms of her employment also allowed her to take a sister for a free education. This was too good an offer to resist and naturally Emily, as the next oldest daughter, was chosen to accompany Charlotte to Mirfield. Within weeks of arriving, however, the painfully shy Emily had become homesick to the point where she had virtually stopped talking and eating. With the demise of her sisters Maria and Elizabeth still on her mind, Charlotte wrote to her father suggesting that if Emily wasn't sent home she would die. Given the family history it's little surprise that Patrick did indeed call Emily back to Haworth, where she made a complete recovery.

The offer of free education still stood, but Patrick and Elizabeth had at first been reticent to send Anne, then 14, to school. In a letter to Anne's godmother Elizabeth Franks (the Elizabeth Firth who had rejected his proposal), Patrick wrote:

'My dear little Anne I intend to keep at home for another year under her Aunt's tuition and my own[14].'

This same letter is also notable for its opening request to Elizabeth, who lived near to Roe Head, to keep a watchful eye on the young Brontës:

'As two of my dear children, are soon to be placed near you, I take the liberty of writing to you a few lines, in order to request both you and Mr. Franks to be so kind, as to interpose with your advice and counsel, to them in any case of necessity – and if expedient to write to Miss Branwell, or me, if our interference should be requisite[15].'

It is significant that Patrick makes Elizabeth Branwell the first point of contact if the Franks should need to write to them regarding the girls, showing that she now had the dominant role in the upbringing of the sisters.

After some discussion between father and aunt, Anne was sent to take Emily's place at Roe Head in October 1835, and as the certificate of 1836 shows it was an environment in which she thrived. Like Emily, and to a lesser degree Charlotte, Anne could be painfully shy in company, yet she battled to overcome this. As well as winning plaudits for her studies she also made a great friend in her fellow pupil Ellen Cook who:

> 'attached herself strongly to Anne B. and Anne bestowed upon her a great deal of quiet affection and genial notice[16].'

Elizabeth was thrilled at the progress her beloved niece was making on both fronts, but she received news of an altogether less welcome kind in late 1837. Anne had suffered a sudden, or at least sudden as far as Charlotte was concerned, physical collapse brought on by mental anguish. Anne had become increasingly worried that she and those she loved were destined for hell, and her troubled mind hastened a physical sickness that culminated in an attack of gastric fever, what we now know as typhoid. It was a frequently deadly condition and we are told that Anne's 'life hung on a slender thread[17]'. At Anne's request, a priest named James la Trobe was called for, and Anne recovered enough to be sent home to Haworth.

Elizabeth is often, unfairly, blamed for Anne's Roe Head breakdown, and for subsequent dark moments of religious doubt that appeared throughout her life. The cause of Anne's fear of hell came not from her aunt, but from the hard-line Calvinist preachers then in abundance in the West Riding of Yorkshire. They believed that sin could never be fully be forgiven, and that once a sin had been committed, the perpetrator was damned to an eternal hell. This was completely at odds with Anne's belief in a loving and forgiving God, and it was a deep examination of these two opposing views that had such a dramatic effect upon her health.

Elizabeth Branwell was far from being a Calvinist, and it was not her religious views that drove her niece to despair. Grimshaw, whom Elizabeth so admired, was a fiery preacher but he believed in a loving God that offered hope for all mankind, as did the leader of his movement John Wesley. In this aspect of doctrine, that of eternal and unforgivable sin, Wesleyans such as Elizabeth were diametrically opposed to the Calvinists. It is notable that, close to death, Anne had asked to speak to James la Trobe rather than the Calvinist priests of the Mirfield area. La Trobe was not a Church of England priest, but a Moravian. The Moravians had originally come to England in exile from central Europe, and they were noted for their belief in the forgiving power of God and a belief in redemption for all. The proximity of Moravian belief to that of Elizabeth Branwell is shown by the fact that Wesley himself, before becoming head of his own movement, associated with the Moravian church[18].

Anne's return to Haworth at the end of 1837 brought an emotional reunion for aunt and niece. We know that both were noted for crying at moments of happiness or sadness, so the tears fell while they hugged each other close. Other than returns for Christmas and summer holidays, Anne had been away from Haworth, and the aunt she'd become so close to, for more than two years.

Elizabeth found that Anne had grown in more than just a physical sense in her time at Roe Head; she was now a learned and eloquent, at least with those she knew, woman, and had found an independent streak as well. Anne's father and siblings were shocked when, just over a year after her return from school, she announced that she intended to find a position as a governess as she wanted to make her way in the world. This was less of a shock to Elizabeth however, who remembered how her sister Maria, Anne's mother, had once taken the same course. In April 1839, Anne was back in Mirfield as governess to the Ingham family of Blake Hall. As anyone who has read *Agnes Grey* knows, this was a far from successful move, as the Ingham children (hidden behind the name of Bloomfield in Anne's novel) were cruel and unwilling to learn. Anne had entertained particularly high hopes for this family as they had been recommended by her aunt Elizabeth who knew that Blake Hall had been a centre of Wesleyanism and often visited by Grimshaw and Wesley alike[19]. Unfortunately, Elizabeth's confidence was misplaced and Anne returned from her first post as governess, disheartened but not defeated, in December 1839.

Elizabeth had missed Anne greatly during her time as a governess and her time at school. She had missed their shared prayers and their discussions on the Bible, and missed the company of a person whose character was so attuned to hers. In those years, however, Elizabeth had found comfort in the company of the other Brontë sibling who held a special place in her heart; a person very different to her youngest niece in many ways.

Chapter 12

Their Darling Truant

'While from the old Rectory, his distant home,
"All hands" to seek their darling truant roam,
And one – his mother – with instinctive love,
Like that which guides aright the timid dove -
Finds her dear child – his cheeks all rain bedewed,
The unconscious victim of those tempests rude,
And, panting, asks him why he tarries there?
Does he not dread his fate – his danger fear?
That child replies – all smiling in the storm -
"Mother – what is this Fear? – I never saw its form!"
Ah! oft, since then, he heard the tempests sound,
Oft saw far mightier waters surging round,
Oft stood unshaken – death and danger near,
Yet saw no more than then the phantom Fear!'
Branwell Brontë, *The Triumph of Mind over Body*

A false yet enduring impression of Elizabeth Branwell is that she was an overly strict woman who did much to halt the enjoyment of her nephew and nieces at Haworth Parsonage, and of those who worked within it. One reason for this is the depiction of her within Elizabeth Gaskell's 1857 biography of her friend Charlotte Brontë:

'Miss Branwell was unaware of the fermentation of unoccupied talent going on around her. She was not her niece's confidante – perhaps no one so much older could have been ... next to her nephew, the docile, pensive Anne was her favourite ... In general, notwithstanding that Miss Branwell might be occasionally unreasonable, she and her nieces went on smoothly enough; and though they might now and then be annoyed at petty tyranny, she still inspired them with sincere respect and not a little affection[1].'

Gaskell's biography of Charlotte Brontë is an important historical document, given that she knew many of the people featured within it, and it's also superbly written, as should be expected from the author of masterpieces such as *Cranford* and *North and South*, but it is also deeply flawed in places. With the passage of time, and access to further documentation and testimonies, it is now acknowledged, for example, that her depiction of Patrick Brontë as a cold, sometimes cruel man is far from the truth. Her assertion that he didn't let his children eat meat and kept them to a rigid and dull diet caused Patrick particular pain, and it's also patently untrue as we have the evidence of servants such as Nancy Garrs to the contrary, and evidence from Emily and Anne Brontë's diary paper of 1835 in which they record:

> 'We are going to have for Dinner Boiled Beef Turnips, potato's and applepudding[2].'

Gaskell also came under fire for a scene in which she depicts Patrick destroying a pair of his wife's shoes, whilst completely misreading his motivation for doing so. On this matter, Ellen Nussey wrote a strongly worded letter to Mrs Gaskell in Patrick's defence:

> 'The anecdote of the little coloured shoes produced a mental sting that no time would obliterate and I feel that all commonplace readers would fail to see the spartan nature of the act unless you plainly pointed it out to them and I was intending to ask you to make very clear and distinct comments on Mr. B's character. I don't wish anything you have said suppressed only I think your readers will have to be taught to think kindly of Mr. B[3].'

Much of Elizabeth Gaskell's inadvertent misinformation regarding Patrick came from the testimony of Martha Wright, the maid who had been dismissed by him and was now settling scores, and we can also see her influence in her depiction of Elizabeth Branwell. Such testimony would have carried even more weight in this case, as while Gaskell knew Patrick Brontë, Elizabeth Branwell had been dead for eight years by the time she made the acquaintance of her niece Charlotte.

Given these factors it is perhaps understandable that Gaskell misrepresented Elizabeth's character and influence upon the Brontës, but it is one that needs correcting. Her depiction given earlier is wholly unfair, not least in its strange assertion that she could not possibly have been the confidante of her charges because of the age difference. Elizabeth Branwell was forty years older than Charlotte, but many children have made confidantes of parents or grandparents with larger age gaps than that. It is possible that, in this instance, Elizabeth Gaskell is projecting her own thoughts and experiences onto siblings that, with the one exception of Charlotte, she didn't know.

Gaskell's early life mirrors that of the Brontës in many respects. Like them, she lost her mother, another Elizabeth, at a very early age; in her case, just thirteen months. Her father, a former clergyman in the Unitarian church, suffered severe mental anguish after the death of his wife, with the result that Elizabeth Stevenson, as she was known before her marriage to William Gaskell, was sent to Knutsford to be raised by her aunt, Hannah Lumb[4]. Under these circumstances, Gaskell's depiction of the Brontës' relationship with their Aunt Branwell may reflect her own relationship with her Aunt Lumb.

There is as little evidence that Elizabeth Branwell was tyrannical as there is for the similar charge against Patrick; indeed, less so, as whilst Reverend Brontë was a kindly and loving father, he admitted in a letter to Elizabeth Gaskell that he could have a warm temper at times:

> 'I do not deny that I am somewhat eccentric. Had I been numbered among the calm, sedate, *concentric* men of the world, I should not have been as I now am, and I should, in all probability never have had such children as mine have been[5].'

In these circumstances, Elizabeth provided much needed discipline to balance Patrick's eccentricity. She was in some ways a perfectionist, and liked to adhere rigidly to a timetable so that Haworth villagers said they would know exactly what the Brontës would be doing at each time of the day[6]. This was far from a tyranny; however, it was a vital necessity within the Brontë household, and her experience with the offspring of her sister, Charlotte Branwell, had taught Elizabeth that all children need boundaries in order to thrive.

When we look beyond the dour image Mrs Gaskell presented of Elizabeth, we find that far from dampening the natural exuberance and fun of the Brontë children, she did much to encourage it, within the boundaries and constraints that she knew needed setting. Elizabeth, far from being the solemn-faced old maid that some imagine, had often a youthful twinkle in her eye, as remembered by Ellen Nussey:

> 'She [Elizabeth Branwell] gave one the idea that she had been a belle among her home acquaintances. She took snuff out of a very pretty gold snuff-box, which she sometimes presented to you with a little laugh, as if she enjoyed the slight shock and astonishment visible in your countenance[7].'

This is not at all what Ellen expected from a lady of her age and status, but Elizabeth is clearly laughing at her own mischief, mischief that she had also enjoyed playing on her siblings during her days as a belle in Penzance. This wicked, yet well-meaning, sense of humour was shared by her niece Emily, as Ellen Nussey again recalled:

> 'A spell of mischief also lurked in her [Emily Brontë] on occasions. When out on the moors she enjoyed leading Charlotte where she would not dare to go of her own free will. C. had a mortal dread of unknown animals and it was Emily's pleasure to lead her into close vicinity and then to tell her of what she had done, laughing at her horror with great amusement[8].'

We now get a picture of parsonage life opposed to the cliched image of a moorside prison, and a heart-warming one it is too, as we see Emily and her aunt Elizabeth laughing conspiratorially in a corner at some little joke they've played.

Ellen Nussey, who has become a primary source of our Brontë knowledge thanks to the huge collection of Charlotte's letters which she kept, was a frequent visitor to the parsonage, and she was warmly welcomed into it by Elizabeth. She could see that her niece's friend was a kind and genuine woman, one who placed loyalty and honesty above all else. These were characteristics also highly prized by Elizabeth, and her admiration for Ellen was demonstrated by a gift she gave to her, and which Ellen treasured. In 1937, C. Mabel Edgerley was herself presented with a gift from a woman who had bought it in a sale many years earlier. It was a parcel wrapped in tissue paper, upon which Ellen Nussey had written 'Mittens knitted by

Miss Branwell, C.B.'s aunt[9]'. Inside the parcel was a pair of beautifully crafted white cotton mittens which must have proved highly useful during winter walks across Haworth's moors.

If Gaskell misrepresented Elizabeth Branwell's character and the impact she had on the Brontë children, she did at least recognise the love that existed between Elizabeth and Branwell. Patrick Branwell Brontë was a troubled individual, especially in later life, and yet whilst others judged him then and now, he was always welcomed by Elizabeth. It is a relationship that once again belies depictions of Elizabeth as cold, strict or dour, and Branwell himself acknowledged the value of her love and support, writing that she 'has for twenty years been as my mother[10].'

From the moment Elizabeth arrived at the parsonage in that sad summer of 1821, she felt drawn to the little red-haired boy, then aged four. He was the only boy in a family of six, just as her brother Benjamin had been the only boy among seven children who survived infancy in the Branwell family. He was a vivacious child, in contrast to his reserved sisters, and Elizabeth saw in him a shadow of the brother she had lost three years before moving to Haworth. Benjamin Branwell had achieved a lot in his forty-three years, from growing a business to starting a family and becoming mayor of his town, so given the right support and encouragement, why shouldn't Branwell Brontë also go on to be a great success in life?

Branwell was largely taught by his father, leaving Elizabeth to concentrate her efforts on her teaching of her nieces, but she liked him to show her his scholarly progress, encouraging his early efforts in poetry, art and music. He was a boy, and later a man, who loved to be praised, and the abundance with which it flowed from his aunt helped to secure her place in his affections.

As always taking a pragmatic view of life, Elizabeth realised the strong possibility that at least some of her nieces would have to rely on the munificence of their brother at some point. Patrick Brontë, in contrast to her own father, would be unable to leave his daughters a meaningful annuity in his will, and in such an unhealthy environment as Haworth there was no telling when he may be snatched away. Alternatively, there was the possibility that Patrick's eyesight or health could fail, leaving him unable to continue his work. By then, Elizabeth reasoned, some of her nieces may have found a husband who could support them, or have found jobs as governesses, although these rarely paid well. If neither of these scenarios had come to pass, it would be up to Branwell to support his sisters. This is why Branwell had to be supported and encouraged at all costs, and his aunt provided props of both the emotional and financial kind.

Elizabeth had good reason to be optimistic about her nephew's future. He had talent and self-confidence, always a winning combination, and he also had a kind heart, drawing pictures for his youngest sister Anne and joining in the games and plays that his siblings loved. Even now, however, there were ominous signs of things to come, and when a dark mood descended Branwell could display a devilish side just as easily as an angelic one.

The first evidence we have of this aspect of Branwell's nature came when Patrick famously lined his children up behind a mask and asked them each a question, figuring that the anonymity provided by the mask would allow them to answer his questions free of their usual reserve. His question to Emily, and her response, is telling:

> 'I asked the next (Emily, afterwards Ellis Bell) what I had best do with her brother Branwell, who was sometimes a naughty boy; she answered, "Reason with him, and when he won't listen to reason, whip him[11]."'

Branwell revelled in the role of maverick outsider throughout his life, and we catch another glimpse of this when he and his sisters chose names for their own personal toy soldiers. Charlotte instantly named hers after her hero the Duke of Wellington, whereupon Branwell decided that his would be Napoleon Bonaparte. Even at this stage of his life – he was then aged eight – he delighted in being the anti-hero rather than the hero. We should also remember, however, that the twelve soldiers had been bought for Branwell, yet he willingly shared them with his sisters; this one early moment encapsulated the duality of his nature.

Clearly Branwell was a child who needed both discipline and understanding in his life, and these were provided by his aunt, creating a close bond between them that was noticed by everyone who saw them together, from Ellen Nussey to Mary Taylor.

Elizabeth was delighted to hear, from her brother-in-law, that Branwell was showing great promise in his lessons, but she was just as happy to indulge his creative side, especially his love of music. He first became proficient on the flute, and then progressed to lessons on the church organ under the tutelage of Mr Sunderland, an organist from Keighley. His promise in this field led to the purchase of an upright cabinet piano originally sold by John Green of Soho Square[12], and it took pride of place in the parsonage at the close of 1833. The purchase of this item would have been beyond the means of Patrick alone, so there can be little doubt that Elizabeth helped to pay for it. It was a purchase that appealed to her for three reasons: firstly it would allow Branwell to hone his keyboard skills so that he could play the organ at church (which he did until he stopped attending services altogether); secondly, it would allow the girls to learn music as well, which could boost their chances of getting a governess's position (Emily became a particularly accomplished pianist); finally, it would allow Elizabeth to hear music being played in the parsonage.

Music and dancing were one of the 'gaities' that Elizabeth remembered so fondly from Penzance, but although the culture, climate and accents of Haworth were alien to her, she was delighted to find that she could still experience live music, even if the setting wasn't always as refined as at the Penzance Assembly Rooms.

Haworth had a thriving music scene, with occasional concerts held at St Michael and All Angels' church and regular performances held at the neighbouring Black Bull Inn, including the annual November the Fifth extravaganza staged by the Haworth Philharmonic Society. These events were attended by all of the parsonage household, but as Patrick was a man of strict habits he always left just before nine in the evening, leaving Elizabeth to chaperone his children and bring them home at the close of the concert.

The concerts were joyous events for all concerned, and we have a contemporary description of one given in the local newspaper:

> 'The Philharmonic Society in this place, held a concert in the Large Room of the Black Bull Inn, on Tuesday evening, April 1st. The songs, catches, and glees were well selected. Miss Parker sung with much sweetness, and was highly applauded. Mr. Parker was in fine voice, and sang with his usual effect. Mr. Clark sung several comic songs with much taste, and was often encored, particularly in the song of "Miss Levi," which kept the audience in continual laughter. The concert was very numerously and respectably attended, and the company went away highly gratified[13].'

It was nights such as these, in the company of their loving aunt, that created the happy memories the Brontës clung to in darker times, particularly in the case of Branwell. By the time of the concert described above, Branwell was 16 years old, but he had already become familiar with another of the delights offered by the Black Bull Inn – whisky. It was not unusual at this time for a young man to drink, indeed as we see from Anne Brontë's *The Tenant of*

Wildfell Hall it was considered an essential quality for a gentleman, and yet Elizabeth, who observed all her sister's children carefully, was worried at the early signs of an over-enthusiasm for the bottle.

Haworth was a dangerous place for a man such as Branwell with an addictive personality, for there were not only three public houses in the vicinity of the parsonage (he would become very familiar with the Black Bull, the White Lion and the King's Arms), there were also houses in the densely packed area known as 'the pick', a shortening of its official name of Piccadilly, that sold home-made spirits and ales. Also known as 'Brandy Row' because it housed a number of brandy and wine merchants[14], it was accessed via the Gauger's Croft archway across from St Michael and All Angels' church. As the years progressed, Branwell replaced attendance at one with frequent visits to the other.

Under these circumstances, Elizabeth conjectured that a change of scenery might do her nephew a power of good, and the opportunity came when he suggested applying to become a student at the Royal Academy of Arts in London. He had been showing great promise as an artist and it was an activity he truly enjoyed, so with the encouragement of his aunt and father he wrote a letter of introduction to the Royal Academy in the summer of 1835[15]. What happened next is far from clear; a witness named Woolven stated that he had seen Branwell later that year in a Holborn tavern[16], but some commentators have opined that Branwell never made the journey at all. What we can say for certain is that Branwell never entered the Academy, and at the close of 1835 he was in Haworth.

Elizabeth had been prepared to subsidise his journey to London, and she also helped to pay for his art lessons with the local artist, teacher and Royal Academy graduate William Robinson[17]. Encouraged by Robinson, Branwell moved to Bradford in May 1838 to start a new career as a portrait painter. It was hardly what Elizabeth had envisaged for her nephew, but, as always, she gave him encouragement and financial backing. Branwell soon discovered that portrait painting at this time was a highly competitive industry, too competitive for a novice like him, one whose art was largely formulaic rather than inspired. Much of his time in the city was spent drinking in haunts such as the Victoria Hotel, and by the time he left his lodgings with Mr and Mrs Kirby in October 1839, he had to pay his debts to them with paintings in lieu of money.

It was another blow on top of his failure to attend the Royal Academy, and now that he was back in Haworth, Elizabeth could see that he was drinking more heavily and regularly. She could not know that his erratic behaviour was also thanks to his new-found love of opium. As she lay in bed at night one recurring thought haunted her; was the nephew she had such high hopes for not at all like her brother Benjamin, but instead like her scandalous brother-in-law John Kingston?

Elizabeth's fears were allayed somewhat when in August 1840 Branwell secured a job as an Assistant Clerk at Sowerby Bridge railway station. Here was a job that brought real prospects, as the fledgling railways were undergoing great expansion at this time. Elizabeth's optimism seemed well founded when her nephew was promoted to the position of chief clerk at Luddendenfoot station four miles west of Halifax just half a year later. It was a time when things were looking bright for the whole family, but the clouds soon returned.

Chapter 13

To Begin a School

'"What was her plan?" A natural one – the next step to be mounted by us, or, at least, by her, if she wanted to rise in her profession. She proposed to begin a school. We already had the means for commencing on a careful scale, having lived greatly within our income. We possessed, too, by this time, an extensive and eligible connection, in the sense advantageous to our business; for, though our circle of visiting acquaintances continued as limited as ever, we were now widely known in schools and families as teachers.'

Charlotte Brontë, *The Professor*

By the middle of 1841, three of the four Brontë siblings were in employment. Branwell, as we have seen, was a chief clerk on the railways, a position that paid well and that offered the prospects of future advancement. Charlotte was at Rawdon, where her mother and father had first met, as governess to the White family. Anne was now in her second governess position, to the Robinson family of the grand Thorp Green Hall near York. Emily had herself had a brief position as teacher at Law Hill school at Southowram near Halifax, but was now back at the parsonage where she had become an excellent baker and housekeeper, as Charlotte readily acknowledged:

'Emily is the only one left at home, where her usefulness and willingness make her indispensable[1].'

Emily was showing great prowess at her domestic duties, which was a relief to both her aunt and father as they knew that her extremely reserved nature would make it difficult for her to obtain a position outside of the parsonage. She was an enigma to Elizabeth, and Emily's character stood in sharp contrast to her aunt's. Whilst Elizabeth had loved to participate in all the joyous events that Penzance had to offer, Emily preferred the company of those she knew and when in the company of strangers, she often remained completely silent. This was as a result of shyness rather than any rudeness or sense of superiority on Emily's part, but it could easily be taken the wrong way by those who didn't know her.

As the years progressed, Emily retreated more and more into the imaginary world of Gondal which she had created with Anne, and her daily walks upon the moors became longer and longer as she enveloped herself in the two things she loved most; nature and her own imagination. Emily's love of nature also found fulfilment in the succession of pets that she and her sisters had throughout their lives. Best known are Emily's dogs Grasper and Keeper, fierce in nature but fiercely loyal to their mistress, and Anne's dog Flossy, a black and white spaniel given to her as a token of appreciation by the Robinson children she governed. There were also rabbits, a succession of cats, geese named Adelaide and Victoria after the royal princesses, and animals that Emily had rescued, injured, from the moor and brought home, including a pheasant, Jasper, and a hawk named Nero.

This was one subject on which aunt and nieces differed, for while Anne and Emily adored animals, Elizabeth thought that a crowded parsonage building was no place in which to keep them. She had an ally in this in Charlotte, as shown in Ellen Nussey's account of her fear of strange animals, but seeing the joy her two youngest nieces got from their pets she let them have their way, especially as they were not overly blessed with companions of the two-legged kind. The collection of parsonage pets was referred to by Anne Brontë in her 1841 diary paper:

> 'We have got Keeper, got a sweet little cat and lost it and also
> got a hawk, got a wild goose which has flown away and 3 tame
> ones, one of which has been killed[2].'

Some have taken this to mean that Elizabeth had the goose killed, but why would she then leave the others alone? A far more likely explanation is that the goose was taken by a poacher or killed by a natural predator.

Another thing Elizabeth found hard to avoid was the collection of writing from her nieces and, at least in his younger years, nephew. From their childhood, she had seen them gather around the dining table, or cluster together at the foot of a bed, as they discussed fantastic plots or read each other their latest poems. Undoubtedly, Elizabeth was sometimes read some of these early literary effusions too, bringing a swell of joy to her heart. She could not fail to mistake the signs of talent in their writing, and although this could never be considered as a potential career, of course, it was a harmless way for them to pass their time. The love of reading that she shared with their father had obviously been taken up by the children as well, and it was now finding an outlet in writing, just as it had with her cousin John Carne.

By this summer of 1841, Elizabeth had been at Haworth parsonage for twenty years. She had witnessed great tragedies, not only the death of her sister but of her two eldest nieces Maria and Elizabeth, snatched away in the midst of childhood. She had also shared moments of laughter and love, and proved a steady guide and financial supporter whenever called upon. Elizabeth had promised to take care of her sister's poor children, and she had not betrayed her oath; they had now grown from a baby and little children to fully grown adults making their way in the world. Each had their own character: Emily was reserved yet fiercely intelligent; Anne was shy but hard-working and determined to overcome her difficulties; Charlotte was fiery and proud, yet kind; and Branwell could be brilliant and funny, although he bore all too clearly the scars of his early childhood losses. Elizabeth had done all she could for them, and she could be proud of the results. Now it was time for them to chart their own passage through life.

Even Patrick now had able assistance to help him with the heavy workload that being Haworth's minister brought. William Weightman was a young man from Westmorland, newly graduated from Durham University, who arrived in Haworth in August 1839 to act as his assistant curate. He was a kind-hearted and learned man who won Patrick's approval during hours spent together debating matters of theology; as we know that Elizabeth too had similar discussions with Patrick, she may also have been present at some of these meetings, and would have been equally impressed.

She was there on the morning of 14 February 1840, when her three nieces received their first ever Valentine's Day cards[3], looking on with a smile as Charlotte, Emily and Anne struggled to contain their excitement. Elizabeth may even have been in on the secret that it took her nieces some hours to discern: the cards (along with a further one for Ellen Nussey who was a guest at the parsonage at the time) had been posted by Weightman who had walked all the way to Bradford in wintry conditions to post them in order to disguise the postmark.

He was obviously a charming man, and greatly loved by the parishioners who later erected a handsome monument in his name[4] - and we only have to remember their attempt to bury Reverend Redhead alive to see how they could be hard to please! As his stay at Haworth proceeded, Elizabeth also discerned a love for him from another source. She sat alongside Anne at church, and couldn't fail to notice what Charlotte had also seen:

> 'He [Weightman] sits opposite Anne at church sighing softly and looking out of the corners of his eyes to win her affection - and Anne is so quiet, her looks so downcast - they are a picture[5].'

Elizabeth knew her niece Anne better than anyone else, and could see that the handsome curate was winning her heart, as much for his good deeds as his good looks. We have seen how Elizabeth was given a place of honour at the Branwell weddings in Penzance, and she now dared to dream of one day attending a similar wedding in Haworth. Why shouldn't it happen? she reasoned to herself: Anne was good hearted, bright and pretty, and there was nothing more natural than for a young curate making his way in the church to select a wife who was the daughter of a more experienced minister.

Elizabeth may even have remained in Haworth partly in anticipation of an eventual union between Anne and William, or at least to give her favourite niece advice and guidance as she took her first steps on the path to love. On the face of it, her work in Haworth was done. Elizabeth had grown accustomed to the local accents, she no longer found the Haworth customs strange, and if the wind was as biting as ever at least it no longer surprised her with its ferocity, and yet at night she could still hear the sea crashing against the rocks of Mount's Bay, could still picture the seagulls wheeling overhead as the latest catch was brought onto the quay. For over two decades she had held onto the dream of returning to the county she called home, and yet even now she remained.

The overriding reason for this inertia was that Elizabeth now looked upon her sister's children as her own. They had brought her love and companionship, along with all the trials and tribulations that also come with raising children, she had never expected to know. She loved them more than her native Cornwall, and however long she had left in life would be spent near them.

It was a fortuitous decision for the Brontës, for all too soon her help was called upon again. In December 1841, Charlotte returned to Haworth having left Rawdon, and even more calamitously in March 1842, Branwell lost his post on the railways, sacked for failing to provide adequate supervision to his subordinates William Spence and Henry Killiner, one of whom had stolen over £11 from the station's accounts[6].

It was a sudden turnaround in fortunes, but Charlotte was now ready to enact a plan that she and her sisters had dreamed of for a long time; they would open their own school. This was despite the fact that Emily's temperament made her unsuited to teach others, as her time at Law Hill had shown, and that Charlotte had found teaching at Roe Head school an almost unbearable strain, as revealed in a series of notes of the time that have become known as her Roe Head Journal. A typical entry from 11 August 1836 reads:

> 'In the afternoon Miss Ellen Lister was trigonometrically ecumenical about her French lessons. She nearly killed me between the violence of the irritation her horrid wilfulness excited and the labour it took to subdue it to a moderate appearance of calmness. My fingers trembled as if I had had twenty four hours tooth-ache, & my spirits felt worn down to a degree of desperate despondency[7].'

Nevertheless the opening of a school was a subject that the three sisters discussed often among themselves – Branwell's unpredictable behaviour meant he could not be considered for this venture – and plans were beginning to become more concrete by the summer of 1841, as revealed in enthusiastic terms by Emily Brontë's diary paper at the end of July:

> 'A scheme is at present in agitation for setting us up in a school
> of our own. As yet nothing is determined but I hope and trust it
> may go on and prosper and answer our highest expectations[8].'

Running their own school would allow the sisters to set their own curriculum and their own rules, and of course they would be there to support each other when needed rather than stranded in the company of strangers. There was one problem, money, and it was the always forthright Charlotte who approached the only hope they had of obtaining the funds they would need, their Aunt Branwell. This was not the little kindnesses Elizabeth had bestowed upon her nephew and nieces down the years, but a substantial sum equivalent to many years' wages for a teacher or governess, and yet as Charlotte revealed in a letter to Ellen, she did not refuse:

> 'To come to the point – Papa & Aunt talk by fits and starts of
> our – id est – Emily, Anne & myself commencing a school!
> I have often you know said how much I wished such a thing

[starting a school] but I never could conceive where the capital would come from for making such a speculation – I was well aware indeed, that Aunt had money – but I always considered that she was the last person who would offer a loan for the purpose in question. A loan however she has offered or rather intimates that she perhaps will offer in case pupils can be secured, an eligible situation obtained etc. etc. This sounds very fair – but still there are matters to be considered which throw something of a damp upon the Scheme. I do not expect that Aunt will risk more than 150£ on such a venture - & would it be possible to establish a respectable (not by any means a shewy) school, and to commence housekeeping with only that amount[9]?'

This is a rather ungenerous response by Charlotte as £150 was three years of her aunt's annuity, and over seven times Charlotte's yearly salary as a teacher at Roe Head school. Elizabeth had also shown her characteristic practicality by advising the sisters to find suitable premises before handing over the money. For a while it looked as if this part of the problem had been solved as Margaret Wooler was selling her school, now at Dewsbury Moor, with a view to retiring. The school was offered to Charlotte at the very reasonable price of £100, and Elizabeth had no hesitation in offering this sum[10], but before the offer could be taken up Charlotte's plans had changed.

Her friend Mary Taylor, along with her sister Martha, was now studying at the Chateau de Koekelberg school in Brussels, and her depiction of the city's splendour in letters to Haworth had woken an urge to travel in Charlotte that superseded any plans for a school at the rather less elegant Dewsbury Moor. The new scheme was presented in a letter sent to her aunt by Charlotte, at that time still in Rawdon, in September 1841:

'Dear Aunt... my friends recommend me, if I desire to secure permanent success, to delay commencing the school for six months longer, and by all means to contrive, by hook or by crook, to spend the intervening time in some school on the continent. They say schools in England are so numerous, competition so great, that without some such step towards attaining superiority we shall probably have a very hard struggle, and may fail in the end. They say, moreover, that the loan of £100, which you have been so kind as to offer us, will, perhaps, not all be required now, as Miss Wooler will lend us the furniture; and that, if the speculation is intended to be a good and successful one, half the sum, at least, ought to be laid out in the manner I have mentioned[11].'

Charlotte then goes on to explain that the cost of the journey would be £5 at most, and that as the cost of living in Belgium is half what it is in England it needn't be a costly venture. She then appeals to her aunt's good nature, while explaining at the same time why one of her nieces would not be partaking in the scheme:

'These are advantages which would turn to vast account, when we actually commenced a school – and, if Emily could share them with me, only for a single half-year, we could take a footing in the world afterwards which we can never do now. I say Emily instead of Anne; for Anne might take her turn at some future period, if our school answered. I feel certain, while I am writing, that you will see the propriety of what I say; you always like to use your money to the best advantage; you are not fond of making shabby purchases; when you do confer a favour, it is often done in style; and depend upon it £50, or £100, thus laid out, would be well employed. Of course, I know no other friend in the world to whom I could apply on the subject except yourself. I feel an absolute conviction that, if this advantage were allowed to us, it would be the making of us for life... I know we have talents, and I want them to be turned to account. I look to you, aunt, to help us. I think you will not refuse... Believe me, dear aunt, your affectionate niece, C. Brontë[12].'

This was a masterful letter from Charlotte, during which she adjusts the £50 to £100 in passing, and appeals to all her aunt's compassion and generosity, but she also has to explain Anne's absence from the Brussels plan. Charlotte realised that Anne was Elizabeth's favourite, and so had to convince her aunt that Anne was is no way being snubbed.

Elizabeth now had a weighty decision to make. She did not approve of Anne's absence, and knew that Charlotte invariably favoured Emily over her youngest sister, but on the other hand, Anne was doing well as a governess to the Robinson family and could continue in that role until her other sisters established a school at some point in the future.

Elizabeth also worried how Charlotte, and especially Emily, would fare in an unknown country; after all, she had witnessed her sister Jane travel to a new land, America, and return in despair months later. Finally, of course, she would miss the companionship of these two nieces, although she would still have Branwell at the parsonage to occupy her time and thoughts.

There were lots of arguments against supporting the scheme, but in spite of all that, Elizabeth was convinced of the common sense within Charlotte's letter, and agreed that an investment now could set them up for life. The happiness of her sister's children was, as always, Elizabeth's priority, and after discussing the matter with Patrick she agreed to pay for Charlotte and Emily to travel to Brussels where they would attend the Pensionnat Heger school. It was a sign of Elizabeth's confidence in her nieces' abilities, and a grand gesture from a financial point of view. Her penultimate grand gesture.

Charlotte, Emily, and Patrick, who accompanied them on their journey to Brussels and who then remained a few days in Belgium before returning to Haworth, arrived in the Belgian capital on 15 February 1842[13].

Anne, still at Thorp Green Hall while her sisters explored the new country without her, now despaired at the prospect of ever opening a Brontë school, and she was dealt a further blow on 6 September 1842, when William Weightman died from cholera, contracted while visiting a sick parishioner. Anne's dreams of love passed with him, and from that moment until the end of her life she wrote a series of powerful poems of love and mourning. Her brother also mourned the assistant curate, as Weightman had become a close companion. Much worse was to follow, as Branwell revealed in an anguished letter to his friend Francis Grundy on 25 October 1842:

> 'I have had a long attendance at the deathbed of the Rev. William Weightman, one of my dearest friends, and now I am attending at the deathbed of my aunt, who has been for twenty years as my mother. I expect her to die in a few hours ... excuse this scrawl, my eyes are too dim with sorrow to see well[14].'

Chapter 14

Rest at Last

'I die but when the grave shall press,
The heart so long endeared to thee,
When earthly cares no more distress,
And earthly joys are nought to me,
Weep not, but think that I have past,
Before thee o'er a see of gloom,
Have anchored safe and rest at last,
Where tears and mourning cannot come.
'Tis I should weep to leave thee here,
On that dark Ocean sailing drear,
With storms around and fears before,
And no kind light to point the shore,
But long or short though life may be,
'Tis nothing to eternity,
We part below to meet on high,
Where blissful ages never die.'

Emily Brontë, *Lines*

Haworth was a growing and increasingly industrialised village at the time Elizabeth Branwell lived there, and life for its inhabitants was frequently tough and short thanks to almost annual epidemics of typhoid and cholera. Indeed, the twenty-one years that Elizabeth spent in the village was longer than the average life expectancy in Haworth during many of the years she spent there[1].

Haworth Parsonage was protected from some of the causes of these diseases as it had its own spring water supply, but the Brontë children in particular often found themselves suffering from colds and flu, especially when the icy winds of winter blew in from the moors. Anne's depiction of this in a letter to Ellen Nussey of January 1848, reflected similar scenes from the preceding years:

'We are all cut up by this cruel east wind, most of us
i.e. Charlotte, Emily, and I have had the influenza or a bad cold

instead, twice over within the space of a few weeks; Papa has
had it once, Tabby has hitherto escaped it altogether[2].'

Nevertheless, their Aunt Elizabeth seemed to enjoy robust health, perhaps
because of the silk shawls she pulled tightly around her or the protective
pattens she clicked around in. Despite being 65 when she waved Charlotte
and Emily off on the first leg of their voyage to Brussels at the start of 1842,
they could have had little idea that they would never see their aunt again.

Mme and M Heger, the man Charlotte fell in love with during her time in
Brussels and who provided inspiration for the Rochester of *Jane Eyre* and Paul
Emanuel of *Villette*, presented their pupils Charlotte and Emily with a letter from
home on 2 November 1842; it was passed from sister to sister with a trembling
hand, and they read in silence the news, from their father, that their aunt had
fallen gravely ill and was not expected to survive. They made immediate plans
to leave the Pensionnat and return to England but on the next morning, as they
were preparing to depart, another letter arrived. The black bordered paper was
all they needed to see for confirmation that their Aunt Branwell was dead.

In fact, Elizabeth Branwell had died, aged 66, on 29 October 1842,
while the letter bringing news of her illness was in transit from Haworth
to Brussels. Branwell's letter of 25 October lamented that she would die
within hours, but in fact she lingered on in terrible pain for another four
days in scenes reminiscent of those Patrick had witnessed with his wife
Maria more than two decades earlier. The official cause of death recorded
on her death certificate was 'exhaustion from constipation[3]', but she died
from a strangulation of the bowel.

Elizabeth's last days consisted of agonising hours drifting from
consciousness to insensibility, but in her lucid moments she remembered how
her beloved sister Maria had met her end in the same fashion, in the same
house, probably the same bed. Her thoughts dwelt once again on her family in
Cornwall, the beautiful coast she would see no more, and then upon her nieces
Charlotte and Emily alone together in a land far away. We do not know if Anne
arrived in time to comfort her aunt, but it seems likely as she was only a day's
travel from Haworth; certainly, she was present at the funeral which was held
five days later. Patrick was by Elizabeth's side reading from the scriptures;
in their time together, they had become more than brother and sister-in-law,
they were close friends, and would have been inseparable companions in old
age. One other man was present, weeping inconsolably by her bed: Branwell
Brontë, judged by others, but always loved by his aunt, had remained by
her side throughout her ordeal. It is his second letter to Francis Grundy that

bears tribute to the finer feelings that he was capable of, and also to the great affection Elizabeth was held in by those who knew her better than anyone:

> 'I am incoherent, I fear, but I have been waking two nights witnessing such agonising suffering as I would not wish my worst enemy to endure; and I have now lost the guide and director of all the happy days connected with my childhood[4].'

Despite the dreadful second letter from their father, Emily and Charlotte continued their voyage home as planned, knowing how much their father, sister and brother now needed them. They arrived in Haworth on 8 November to a house still silently reeling. There were no more sounds of pattens on stone, the only noise now came from the steady ticking of the grandfather clock.

The returning sisters had missed their aunt's funeral held on the third of November, and presided over by Rev James Bradley from the neighbouring parish of Oakworth[5], but they were all too familiar with her place of rest. Visitors to Haworth's St Michael and All Angels' church today may notice an inscription upon a pillar near the altar; it reads:

> 'The Brontë family vault is situated below this pillar, near to the place where the Brontë's pew stood in the old church. The following members of the family were buried here Maria and Patrick, Maria, Elizabeth, Branwell, Emily Jane, Charlotte.'

Anne is missing from this memorial as she died, and was buried, in Scarborough, but there is another person missing whose name should be there, for also in that vault lies eternally Elizabeth Branwell, buried, as per her wishes, 'as near as convenient to the remains of my dear sister[6].'

This provision was stipulated by Elizabeth Branwell at the start of her will made on 30 April 1833, before witnesses William Brown (brother of the Haworth sexton John Brown,) his son William Brown Jr., and John Tootill, in which she also asks that, 'my funeral shall be conducted in a moderate and decent manner[7].'

Following these instructions for her funeral and burial place, Elizabeth then laid out her legacy, and it was one that changed literary history:

> 'My Indian workbox I leave to my niece Charlotte Brontë; my workbox with a China top I leave to my niece Emily Jane Brontë,

together with my ivory fan; my Japan dressing-box I leave to my nephew Patrick Branwell Brontë; to my niece Anne Brontë, I leave my watch with all that belongs to it; as also my eyeglass and its chains, my rings, silver-spoons, books, clothes, etc., etc., I leave to be divided between my above-named three nieces, Charlotte Brontë, Emily Jane Brontë, and Anne Brontë, according as their father shall think proper. And I will that all the money that shall remain, including twenty-five pounds sterling, being the part of the proceeds of the sale of my goods which belong to me in consequence of my having advanced to my sister Kingston the sum of twenty-five pounds in lieu of her share of the proceeds of the goods aforesaid, and deposited in the bank of Bolitho Sons and Co., Esqrs., of Chiandower, near Penzance, after the aforesaid sums and articles shall have been paid and deducted, shall be put into some safe bank or lent on good landed security, and there left to accumulate for the sole benefit of my four nieces, Charlotte Brontë, Emily Jane Brontë, Anne Brontë, and Elizabeth Jane Kingston; and this sum or sums, and whatever other property I may have, shall be equally divided between them when the youngest of them living shall have arrived at the age of twenty-one years[8].'

By the time of Elizabeth's death in 1842, all four named nieces had reached 21 years of age and so they received the considerable sum of £300 each, or around six times the annual wage that Anne Brontë was receiving from the Robinson family. This put an end to any immediate money concerns the cousins in Yorkshire and Cornwall had.

Branwell was left the Japan dressing-box but no money in his aunt's will, but this shouldn't be taken as a slight upon a nephew that she truly loved. At the time the will was written in 1833, Elizabeth had no doubt that Branwell would go on to forge a successful career and would therefore be in little need of her money. The fact that Elizabeth didn't amend her will in the nine years after this indicates that she still had high hopes of him securing a stable future for himself.

In the midst of their grief there was now a lot for the Brontë sisters to discuss. It was eventually agreed that Emily would remain at Haworth parsonage to take over the running of the household, this being the period when Tabby was at her sister's house, and the only servant living there at the time was 14-year-old Martha Brown. Anne would, reluctantly, return to her post as governess at Thorp Green Hall, and Charlotte insisted upon returning to Brussels where she had been given the option of serving as a teacher at the Pensionnat Heger while furthering her education. The dream of opening a school was still at the forefront of their minds, and they now had the funds to make it happen.

All seemed set for a positive resolution to this scheme, but things soon went wrong on all fronts, pushing the sisters into a very different future. Without Emily's calming influence beside her, Charlotte let her emotional attachment to her married professor loose, and with this came a gradual loathing of his wife, and her employer, Madame Claire Heger. Things could not continue as they were, and Charlotte announced her decision in a letter to Emily:

> 'Dear E.J., I have taken my determination. I hope to be at home the day after New Year's Day... Low spirits have affected me much lately, but I hope all will be well when I get home... I am not ill in body. It is only the mind which is a trifle shaken – for want of comfort. I will try to cheer up now[9].'

As 1844 dawned, Charlotte was back in Haworth, dejected and heartbroken. Emily was there to comfort her in her usual thoughtful, if quiet way, but Branwell had now joined his sister Anne at Thorp Green Hall. Anne, mindful of his struggles to find work and always willing to give those she loved another chance, had persuaded the Robinsons to employ her brother as tutor to their son Edmund Robinson junior. Greatly impressed with Anne, and hoping that her brother would be cut from the same cloth, the Robinsons agreed to this proposal, but it was a terrible mistake all round. Branwell soon fell in love with the middle-aged mistress of the house, Lydia Robinson, and embarked upon an affair with her, although the extent to which this affair was carried out will remain a mystery. Anne, ashamed that she had unwittingly facilitated this unholy relationship, resigned her post in June 1845, after more than five years of exemplary service, and returned to Haworth in low spirits. A month later Branwell was back too, dismissed by the choleric Edmund Robinson, who perchance had discovered the secret without Anne there to temper her brother's excesses.

Suddenly, all four Brontë children were once again in the parsonage and without paid employment, and it was time once more to turn to the plan of opening their own school. Cards were printed for the 'Misses Brontë Establishment for the Board and Education of a Limited Number of Young Ladies' and a curriculum put together that included lessons in needlework, writing, arithmetic, history, grammar, and geography as well as optional lessons in languages, music and drawing. The advertised cost of £35 per year was, however, prohibitively expensive for a not-yet established school, especially one in a village as remote and unhealthy as Haworth. Their efforts and dreams that had first been supported by their Aunt Branwell four years earlier had come to nothing; not one pupil could be secured for their proposed school.

The sisters' revised plans had been to modify the parsonage building and hold lessons there, but they must have known that this too brought an insurmountable problem in the form of their brother Branwell. Without the controlling influence of his aunt his addictions to drink and opium had strengthened, and his mood swings, by turn raging and self-pitying, made the parsonage no place to teach young ladies.

This was a moment of crisis for the Brontës. Although Elizabeth's legacy would sustain them financially for a number of years there seemed little chance of them turning their talents to account, as Charlotte had put it in her letter to her aunt. A sudden discovery, chance or otherwise, changed everything:

> 'One day, in the autumn of 1845, I [Charlotte Brontë] accidentally lighted on a manuscript volume of verse in my sister Emily's handwriting. Of course, I was not surprised, knowing that she could and did write verse: I looked it over, and something more than surprise seized me, - a deep conviction that these were not common effusions, not at all like the poetry women generally write. I thought them condensed and terse, vigorous and genuine. To my ear, they also had a peculiar music - wild, melancholy, and elevating[11].'

Charlotte knew that her sisters were both prolific poets, and they often read her their poems set in Gondal, that invented land of adventure, romance and deceit. What Charlotte now had in her hands was something very different; this was Emily's hidden poetry book, containing deep, visionary and often dark poems about faith, nature, death and the art of creation. They were a key to Emily's soul, and she was furious when she learned Charlotte had found them. After days of silent, and not so silent, recriminations, Anne managed to persuade Emily of the opportunity the discovery had brought. This was a chance, perhaps their final chance, to do something with their lives and with the talents they all possessed. Calmed and convinced by the words of the sister she loved more than anything in the world, Emily finally agreed to their plan; they would put together a collection of poems, each sister having broadly equal representation, and send it out into the world to find a publisher.

Although grudgingly agreeing to this scheme, Emily insisted upon taking the precaution of adopting pen names; having her most heartfelt poems read and judged by her sisters was bad enough, she could not bear the thought of them being placed before strangers. The adoption of pen names also served another purpose, as Charlotte explained in the post-mortem biographical notice of her sisters:

> 'We did not like to declare ourselves women, because we had a vague impression that authoresses are liable to be looked on with prejudice[12].'

The names selected by the sisters are revealing. Whilst keeping their own initials, Charlotte became Currer Bell, probably inspired by Frances Richardson-Currer, the woman who had provided financial help to her father in his hour of need, and whom Charlotte may have met during her brief spell as a governess at Stone Gappe, a neighbouring property to Eshton Hall. Emily became Ellis Bell, with Ellis presumably a shortened tribute to the two Elizabeths she had loved and lost, her tragic sister and her Cornish aunt. Anne chose Acton Bell, and the inspiration for this may be the castle her aunt had told her about during many childhood stories, the castle just outside Penzance that was clearly visible from the Branwell house on Chapel Street, Acton Castle. It is often conjectured that the surname Bell was inspired by the sound of bells from their father's church; this may be so, but it could also be a contraction of the family name B(ranw)ell.

The collection of sixty-one poems was entitled *Poems by Currer, Ellis and Acton Bell* and it was sent with diminishing hope to a selection of publishers. It seemed as if no-one was interested in this collection of verse by unknown brothers, until they received a letter from poetry specialists Aylott & Jones of Paternoster Row, London. They agreed that the work showed promise, but insisted on an up-front payment of thirty five pounds, eighteen shillings and three pence to publish it[13].

It was a large sum that four years earlier would have been simply beyond their reach, but they now had the money left them by their aunt to call upon. The discussion now was whether this was a sensible way to invest part of their legacy, and whether such a speculative move would have been approved of by their aunt? The answer was clear. Elizabeth would have supported them whatever they chose to do, and would have had confidence in the success of their venture. The money was sent and in May 1846, the first book by the Brontë sisters was published. Made possible by their Aunt Branwell's money, it would not, of course, be their last venture into print.

Chapter 15

Last Days

'Rachel admitted me into the parlour, and went to call her mistress, for she was not there: but there was her desk left open on the little round table beside the high backed chair, with a book laid upon it. Her limited but choice collection of books was almost as familiar to me as my own; but this volume I had not seen before. I took it up. It was Sir Humphry Davy's "Last Days of a Philosopher", and on the first leaf was written "Frederick Lawrence." I closed the book, but kept it in my hand, and stood facing the door, with my back to the fire-place, calmly waiting her arrival.'

Anne Brontë, *The Tenant of Wildfell Hall*

Elizabeth's legacy had provided the money that allowed the Brontë sisters, under their aliases of Currer, Ellis and Acton Bell, to finally see their work in print, and now, after paying a further £2 for advertising costs[1], they waited with mixed feelings to see how their collection of poetry would be received.

Initial omens looked promising, as the book received relatively positive reviews from both *The Critic* and the *Athenaeum*, who referred to the 'brothers', as they supposed them to be, as 'a family in whom appears to run the instinct of song[2]'. They even received a request for autographs, forwarded by their publisher. Unfortunately, this fan of their work, a Mr. Frederick Enoch of Warwick[3], was initially one of only two people to purchase this collection.

It could be expected that Charlotte, Emily and Anne would be despondent at this complete and utter failure of their poetry, but a famous letter sent from Charlotte to a number of famous writers at the time (including Thomas de Quincey and Alfred Tennyson) suggests otherwise:

'My relatives, Ellis and Acton Bell and myself, heedless of the repeated warnings of various respectable publishers, have committed the rash act of publishing a volume of poems. The consequences predicted have, of course, overtaken us; our book is found to be a drug; no man needs it or heeds it; in the space of a year our publisher has disposed of but two copies, and by what painful efforts he succeeded in disposing of those two, himself only knows. Before transferring the edition to the trunkmakers, we have decided on distributing as presents a few copies of what we cannot sell[4].'

This letter has a jocular tone, for whilst the Brontës had failed to enjoy the success they had hoped for with *Poems by Currer, Ellis and Acton Bell*, they had rediscovered their childhood love of writing together, and it is this that galvanised them into embarking upon another scheme of writing.

Poetry was a shared love of the Brontës, but they now realised that if they were to make any money out of writing they would have to turn to prose. The halcyon days of poetry, with the likes of Byron and Scott selling vast quantities of their work, were over; even sales of the great Wordsworth were down. Novels, on the other hand, were beginning to enjoy a boom, thanks to their increasing affordability and the popularity of circulating libraries. It should be noted, however, that despite Charlotte's light-hearted prediction, the sisters' poetry was not pulped and recycled into trunk lining; the publishing house Smith, Elder & Co later bought the unsold stock from Aylott & Jones and sold every last copy, after which they sent Charlotte royalties of twenty-four pounds and six pence[5].

A succinct summary of what happened next was given by Charlotte in her short biography of her sisters:

'Ill-success failed to crush us: the mere effort to succeed had given a wonderful zest to existence; it must be pursued. We each set to work on a prose tale: Ellis Bell produced *Wuthering Heights*, Acton Bell *Agnes Grey*, and Currer Bell also wrote a manuscript in one volume. These MSS. were perseveringly obtruded upon various publishers for the space of a year and a half; usually, their fate was an ignominious and abrupt dismissal. At last *Wuthering Heights* and *Agnes Grey* were accepted on terms somewhat impoverishing to the two authors[6].'

The sisters had originally suggested to publishers that their offerings could be published together as a three volume set, at the time the most popular way to publish a book. Unfortunately, Charlotte's contribution, *The Professor,* was not up to the standard of her future endeavours and was only published posthumously. It had been agreed before sending their manuscripts on their long journeys that, this time, they would not pay to have them published as they had with their poetry, but as Charlotte hints above the actuality was somewhat different.

Thomas Cautley Newby wrote to Emily and Anne, or Ellis and Acton as he knew them, in July 1847, offering to publish their novels if they paid him an initial fee of £50. This fee would be repaid once Newby had made that figure through their sales. Even under this deal he had no interest in publishing *The Professor*, which may have jaundiced Charlotte somewhat as she was bitterly opposed to her sisters paying the sum. Pay him they did, however, thanks to the reserves of money they had from Elizabeth's will, and without which the wild brilliance of *Wuthering Heights* and the gentle beauty of *Agnes Grey* would still be unknown.

Elizabeth's influence on the Brontë's novels is not only shown in the fact that they exist at all, but is also apparent within their content, for she can be seen in every one of them. In *Wuthering Heights,* for example, we hear echoes of Aunt Branwell's stories of Penzance, from tales of ghosts walking at night to a grieving man scraping away the earth from the coffin of his beloved.

Charlotte did not let the failure of *The Professor* deter her and encouraged by the response from one publisher, the aforementioned Smith, Elder & Co., she quickly finished and then submitted her second novel. It was *Jane Eyre*, and so enamoured of it were the publishers that it was available to the public in October 1847, two months before *Wuthering Heights* and *Agnes Grey* reached the shelves.

Charlotte had spent less time with Elizabeth Branwell throughout her life than either Emily or Anne, and yet in *Jane Eyre* she does not fail to acknowledge the debt that she and her sisters owed to their aunt:

> "'Briggs is in London. I should doubt his knowing anything at all about Mr Rochester; it is not in Mr Rochester he is interested. Meantime, you forget essential points in pursuing trifles: you do not enquire why Mr Briggs sought after you – what he wanted with you."
>
> "'Well what did he want?"

> "'Merely to tell you that your uncle, Mr Eyre of Madeira, is dead; that he has left you all his property, and that you are now rich – merely that – nothing more[6].'"

This inheritance from an uncle provides Jane the opportunity to dream of something more than being a governess or teacher for the rest of her life, just as Aunt Branwell's will had allowed Charlotte to pursue her own dream, now with spectacular success. Of course, Elizabeth's gift of £300 was rather less than Uncle John Eyre's £20,000, but it had been more than enough to free Charlotte from any immediate need to seek another demoralising job.

Elizabeth is most present, as is to be expected, in the work of the niece she was closest to, Anne. In *Agnes Grey* we see her both as Aunt Grey and as the mother figure who eventually opens a school with Agnes by the coast.

Anne's second novel, *The Tenant of Wildfell Hall*, has the titular heroine, Helen, being raised by her uncle and aunt. It is Helen's aunt that gives her advice on the perils and snares of love, just as Elizabeth surely did at some time with Anne:

> "'Remember Peter, Helen! Don't boast, but *watch*. Keep a guard over your eyes and ears as the inlets of your heart, and over your lips as the outlet, lest they betray you in a moment of unwariness. Receive, coldly and dispassionately, every attention, till you have ascertained and duly considered the worth of the aspirant; and let your affections be consequent upon approbation alone[7].'"

We have already seen how Helen's decision to leave her abusive husband, Arthur, reflected the action taken by Anne's Aunt Jane who left her husband John Kingston in America and returned to Cornwall with her youngest child. There is one other, subtle, tribute to Penzance, and by association to the aunt that she loved, in *The Tenant of Wildfell Hall*, and it is contained at the head of this chapter. As a pivotal moment of the novel approaches, Gilbert Markham finds a book on Helen's reading desk. Anne is careful to reveal the name of the book, although it has no further relevance to the plot; it is by Sir Humphry Davy, the Penzance native known, and often spoken about, by her aunt.

Elizabeth's praise of her fellow townsman had encouraged Anne to seek out Davy's works and she rated him very highly, as we can see from the following extract in Anne's unfinished treatise in the Brotherton Library archives:

> 'Let us take Sir Humphry Davy's theory, found in his last days of a philosopher: I know not any more sensible or philosophical view of the Geological history of the last stages of the world we inhabit, and it contains not one statement that actually contradicts the concise and simple account given by Moses[8].'

The essay then proceeds to an in-depth discussion of geological evolution, explaining how it is compatible with the teachings of the Bible. After eleven pages it comes to a sudden halt, after which the notebook is reversed and used by Arthur Bell Nicholls to transcribe some of his wife Charlotte's poetry. This provenance, the cessation mid-essay of Anne's writing, and its link via Davy to *The Tenant of Wildfell Hall*, makes me suspect that it may be the last prose writing ever created by Anne Brontë.

The Tenant of Wildfell Hall proved a great success, but it was also a highly controversial novel, dealing unflinchingly with themes such as addiction, infidelity and marital cruelty. This led to a savage critical reception, with *The Rambler* noting that:

> 'The scenes which the heroine portrays in her diary are of the most disgusting and revolting species[9].'

Unfortunately for Anne, this was a view that her sister Charlotte shared too. In 1850, Smith, Elder & Co. were planning on re-issuing the three novels written by her sisters, but Charlotte wrote to W.S. Williams of the firm and stated that:

> '"Wildfell Hall" it hardly appears to me desirable to preserve. The choice of subject in that work is a mistake – it was too little consonant with the character, tastes and ideas of the gentle, retiring, inexperienced writer[10].'

Charlotte, as she often did, had misunderstood her youngest sister's character and greatly downplayed the worldliness of a woman who spent longer in employment than the rest of her siblings put together, but her verdict on *The Tenant of Wildfell Hall* stuck. It would not be re-published for another decade. Charlotte's disdain for her sister's book may have been because she was jealous of the attention, and sales, it was getting, or it may have been that its frank portrayal of alcoholism hit too close to home in a household where Branwell's addictions were spiralling out of control. One thing she could not have known is that *The Tenant of Wildfell Hall* was about to inadvertently bring tragedy to the parsonage in triplicate.

On the morning of 7 July 1848, a letter addressed to Currer Bell arrived bearing a London postmark. Upon opening it, Charlotte found a letter from her publisher George Smith that caused her terrible anguish. The contents of this missive, and their effect upon the recipient, were recollected by Smith in his memoirs:

> 'We were met during the negotiations with our American correspondents by the statement that Mr. Newby had informed them that he was about to publish the next book by the author of 'Jane Eyre,' under her other *nom de plume* of Acton Bell – Currer, Ellis and Acton Bell being in fact, according to him, one person. We wrote to 'Currer Bell' to say that we should be glad to be in a position to contradict the statement, adding at the same time we were quite sure Mr. Newby's assertion was untrue. Charlotte Brontë has related how the letter affected her. She was persuaded that her honour was impugned[11].'

Both Anne and Charlotte knew instantly that their honesty was being questioned thanks to Anne and Emily's publisher Thomas Cautley Newby's unscrupulous approach to business. For Charlotte there was the added trauma of being thought the author of *The Tenant of Wildfell Hall*, the novel being offered to American publishers by Newby, and a book she considered an entire mistake.

There was only one way they could disprove Newby's assertion and regain their honour, although it seemed a monstrous move; they would have to travel to London to meet their publishers face-to-face. The time for anonymity was over. Emily gave her consent as long as her identity remained secret, and it is a mark of Charlotte and Anne's fury at Newby that they set out for London that very day.

Modes of transport had come a long way in the twenty-seven years since Elizabeth Branwell had taken over a week to journey from Penzance to Haworth; the railway system was transforming the nation, and now her nieces caught the 7.55pm train from Leeds, arriving at London Euston at 4.30am the next day, after stops at stations including Barnsley, Sheffield and Rugby[12].

Their first task was an unpleasant but necessary one, as, after moving into their lodgings at the Chapter Coffee House behind St Paul's Cathedral (where Charlotte had stayed with Emily and her father en route to Brussels), they made their way to the Smith, Elder & Co. offices at Cornhill near the Bank of England. Naive as to the ways of business, the sisters had not suspected that the proprietor may be away from his office on what was a Saturday morning, but luckily for them he was in place behind his desk. Smith, a young man who had recently inherited the business, was amazed at the two small, timid women who presented themselves, and was then more than amazed at their story. Charlotte was made to sign her signature, as Currer Bell, and it was at last clear that here, after all, were the feted Currer and Acton Bell; not two mysterious brothers, but a clergyman's daughters.

The sisters had planned to return to Yorkshire the next day, but Smith would hear nothing of it. He and his assistant, W.S. Williams, the man who'd first spotted the brilliance of *Jane Eyre* and who became a regular correspondent of Charlotte, showed them some of the most splendid sights of London over the next three days: from the Royal Italian Opera at Covent Garden to Kensington Gardens and the splendid St Stephen's church in Walbrook; they even saw the magnificent art collection at the Royal Academy, which was probably more than their brother had managed. Charlotte would visit London several times in the coming years, but this was to be Anne's only journey outside of Yorkshire, other than moorland walks with Emily that sometimes saw her cross the nearby Lancashire border. It was a joyous four days for Anne, where she experienced the gaieties of society life that her aunt had often told her about. From these four happy days, however, sprang eight desperate months.

By mid-1848 Branwell Brontë's alcohol and opium addiction had reached epic proportions thanks to the absence of Elizabeth's controlling influence and his despair over the break-up of his relationship with Lydia Robinson, who had by then been widowed, and was months away from remarrying and becoming Lady Scott[13]. His behaviour was increasingly erratic; he at one point set fire to his own bed after falling asleep with a candle, and for his own safety he now slept with his aged father. Branwell's death aged 31 on September 25 may not then seem surprising, but the cause of it was, for he died not as a result of alcohol or opium, but of tuberculosis.

Emily soon showed signs of the disease as well, becoming racked with pain and terribly emaciated. With her typical bravery, and typical stubbornness, she resisted all attempts to help her, and Charlotte wrote to Ellen despairingly to say:

'She resolutely refuses to see a doctor; she will give no explanation of her feelings, she will scarcely allow her illness to be alluded to. Our position is, and has been for some weeks, exquisitely painful. God only knows how all this is to terminate. More than once have I been forced boldly to regard the terrible event of her loss as possible and even probable. But Nature shrinks from such thoughts. I think Emily seems the nearest thing to my heart in this world[14].'

The terrible event in question came to pass on 19 December. The worried eyes of Charlotte and Patrick now turned to Anne, and the racking coughs and blood-stained handkerchief showed that she too had tuberculosis. Unlike Emily, Anne tried all the medical cures available, to no avail, and on 24 May 1849, she began her final journey – to Scarborough in the company of Charlotte and their kind, faithful friend Ellen Nussey.

Anne had visited Scarborough, on the North Yorkshire coast, every summer during her five years as governess to the Robinson family, and she fell rapidly in love with what was then a very fashionable resort. Her final hours, as recounted lovingly by Ellen, were spent sat by the window of 2, The Cliff, Wood's Lodgings. Anne was contemplating death, and the life to come, but she was also taking one last look at the sea she loved so much. She paid homage to it in a number of her poems, and in both her novels, such as this passage from *Agnes Grey*:

'The sea was my delight; and I would often gladly pierce the town to obtain the pleasure of a walk beside it, whether with the pupils or alone with my mother during the vacations. It was delightful to me at all times and seasons, but especially in the wild commotion of a rough sea-breeze, and in the brilliant freshness of a summer morning[15].'

Anne Brontë died aged 29 on 28 May 1849. In a rapid space of time tuberculosis had claimed three members of the same family, and yet it was not a disease common in Haworth but rather one of big cities such as London. In the opinion of Professor Philip Rhodes it was Charlotte and Anne's visit to London in July 1848, that brought the disease to the parsonage with devastating results:

'[Emily] might have collected an overwhelming dose of tubercle bacilli from Branwell. She seems to have been the practical one about the household and may well have been Branwell's nurse and so liable to massive infection... It is of especial interest that Charlotte and Anne made a hurried journey to London in July, 1848... Could one or other of the sisters have picked up a further dose of tubercle bacilli which when they returned to Haworth they handed on to Branwell and to Emily? This seems a most likely supposition. Almost certainly one or other of them introduced a new pathogenic element into the closed community of Haworth Parsonage, which wreaked so much havoc so quickly[16].'

Anne was buried in St Mary's churchyard at the foot of Scarborough Castle, overlooking the sea she adored. She had never reached Penzance, but as a child had heard glorious stories of the majesty of the sea around it. Scarborough became Anne's Penzance substitute; it was where she could feel closest to her beloved Aunt Branwell, even in her final moments.

Chapter 16

Connections in the South

'Insuperable embarrassment seized Caroline when this demand was made: she could not, and did not attempt to comply with it. Her silence was immediately covered by Mrs. Pryor, who proceeded to address sundry questions to Mr. Helstone regarding a family or two in the neighbourhood, with whose connections in the south she said she was acquainted.'

Charlotte Brontë, *Shirley*

In July 1848, Charlotte Brontë had received the fateful letter from George Smith that sent her and Anne to London, leaving her sister Emily and brother Branwell behind in Haworth. By the start of June 1849, all but she were dead, and her steps now echoed around the parsonage as she continued to walk round and round the dining table at evening time, just as she had when there were others to share her perambulation.

This was a time of mourning for her father too, who now had just one of his six children to comfort him in his old age. Other than Charlotte and Patrick, there was also the young servant Martha Brown and the old servant Tabby Ayckroyd, who had now returned to the parsonage. For Charlotte, it was a building full of ghosts; her mother who had left her when she was just five years old, the eldest sisters Maria and Elizabeth she had looked up to, Aunt Branwell whose pattens clicked no more, the pitiful brother she had once loved, and now the two sisters she had shared her dream of writing with. A walk upon the moors always brought them to her mind, and just looking at their poetry was enough to make her think of taking one final, terrible step:

'I am free to walk on the moors - but when I go out there alone everything reminds me of the time when others were with me and then the moors seem a wilderness, featureless, solitary, saddening. My sister Emily had a particular love for them, and there is not a knoll of heather, not a branch of fern, not a young bilberry leaf not a fluttering lark or linnet but reminds me of her. The distant prospects were Anne's delight, and when I look round, she is in the blue tints, the pale mists, the waves and shadows of the horizon. In the hill-country silence their poetry comes by lines and stanzas into my mind: once I loved it - now I dare not read it - and am driven often to wish I could taste one draught of oblivion and forget much that, while mind remains, I never shall forget[1].'

Amidst her loneliness and despair, however, Charlotte remembered the final exhortation of her sister Anne: 'Take courage, Charlotte, take courage![2]' Finding solace in the work she had put aside, Charlotte completed her third novel *Shirley* (the second to be published of course) which had been half finished at the time her brother and sisters fell ill.

Shirley is an unfairly overlooked novel, and it is of particular interest to Brontë lovers as many of the characters are based upon people that the author knew intimately. The Yorke family of Briarmains, for example, represent the Taylors of the Red House at Gomersal. The eponymous Shirley Keeldar is an alternative imagining of Emily Brontë, as Charlotte revealed to Elizabeth Gaskell:

'The character of Shirley herself, is Charlotte's representation of Emily... we must remember how little we are acquainted with her, compared to that sister who, out of her more intimate knowledge, says that she "was genuinely good, and truly great," and who tried to depict in Shirley Keeldar, as what Emily Brontë would have been, had she been placed in health and prosperity[3].'

Shirley may have the novel named after her, but she does not appear until a quarter of the book is over, so the true heroine of the story can be said to be Caroline Helstone, based upon Anne Brontë. At the commencement of the book, she is being raised by her uncle, the Reverend Matthewstone Helstone. It is commonly thought that Charlotte had planned to kill off the character of Caroline, but by the time she came to that point in the novel Anne had died. Unable to save her sister in real life Charlotte did save her in print, and so whilst we see Caroline seemingly dying of a tuberculosis-like disease, she miraculously recovers, partly thanks to the loving attention of Mrs Pryor.

Mrs Pryor is an older woman who has come to Yorkshire from the south, and is now acting as governess to Shirley. It is in this character that we see a portrayal of Elizabeth Branwell, and during Caroline's struggle for life it is revealed that Mrs Pryor is in fact her long lost mother. In this we hear a memory of the conversations Charlotte heard her aunt have with Anne, and a tribute to the loving relationship they had together in which the aunt had become a surrogate mother to the niece who shared her room:

> 'The evening restored Caroline entirely to her mother, and Mrs. Pryor liked the evening; for then, alone with her daughter, no human shadow came between her and what she loved. During the day she would have her stiff demeanour and cool moments, as was her wont. Between her and Mr. Helstone a very respectful but most rigidly ceremonious intercourse was kept up... Towards the servants Mrs. Pryor's bearing was not uncourteous, but shy, freezing, ungenial[4].'

One passage in *Shirley* reminds us of Ellen's description of Elizabeth Branwell habitually wearing the same black silk dress; Caroline asks Mrs Pryor to buy other clothes to wear as well as the black silk dress she always dons, but Mrs Pryor says that she would rather spend the money on Caroline, to which she replies:

> 'People say you are miserly; and yet you are not, for you give liberally to the poor and to religious societies – though your gifts are conveyed so secretly and quietly that they are known to few except the receivers[5].'

Charlotte completed just one more book after *Shirley*, her Belgium based novel *Villette*, which borrowed from, and vastly improved upon, her first novel *The Professor*. The Heger-like Professor Emanuel looms large throughout its pages, but at its heart it is another story about the importance of family and roots: with a godmother, Mrs Bretton, taking on the mother-role this time.

Now that her family were gone, all but her father, Charlotte's thoughts were increasingly occupied with memories of them, and in September 1851, an event occurred that once again brought the Brontë and Branwell families together: a visit from Thomas Brontë Branwell[6], the 34-year-old son of the woman Charlotte Brontë had been named after, Charlotte Branwell. The reason for his visit remains unknown, although he may have been in Yorkshire for business reasons. It may also be that he'd come to visit his cousin Charlotte now that he knew she was a celebrated author, and he may even have had romantic intentions; he was after all unmarried and a year younger than Charlotte, and his father and mother (who had died three years earlier) had themselves been cousins.

Thomas stayed in Haworth for around a week, and doubtless he visited the resting place of his Aunt Elizabeth who had nursed him as a child, although as she left Penzance when he was four he had little recollection of her. This visit of Thomas may be the source of some of the Brontë family relics and papers that came into the hands of the Branwell family, mementoes given by Patrick to the nephew of his long-departed, but much-loved, wife.

Charlotte seemed relieved when her cousin departed once more for Penzance, as she wrote to her erstwhile teacher, employer, and now firm friend Margaret Wooler to say:

> 'Our visitor (a relative from Cornwall) having left us, the coast is now clear, so that whenever you feel inclined to come, papa and I will be truly glad to see you[7].'

This is not necessarily a slight against cousin Thomas, merely a wish to see Margaret again who was now living in Scarborough. Less ambiguous was Charlotte's reaction to the only other recorded visit of a Branwell relative to the parsonage. At the start of August 1840, John Branwell Williams and his family came to Haworth to spend time with John's cousin Elizabeth. It must have been delightful for Elizabeth to hear that familiar, almost forgotten, accent again and to catch up on the latest news from Penzance. Charlotte, however, was now all too acutely aware of the difference in their social status, as revealed in a letter to Ellen:

> 'We had, a fortnight ago, a visit from our South of England relations, John Branwell and his wife and daughter... They reckon to be very grand folks indeed, and talk largely – I thought assumingly. I cannot say I much admired them. To my eyes there seemed to be a great attempt to play the Mogul down in Yorkshire. Mr. Branwell was much less assuming than the womenites; he seemed a frank, sagacious kind of man, very tall and vigorous, with a keen active look. The moment he saw me he exclaimed that I was the very image of my Aunt Charlotte. Mrs. Branwell sets up for being a woman of great talent, tact and accomplishment. I thought there was much more noise than work. My cousin Eliza is a young lady intended by nature to be a bouncing, good-looking girl... I would have been friendly with her, but I could get no talk except about

the Low Church, Evangelical clergy, the Millennium, Baptist Noel, botany, and her own conversion. A mistaken education has utterly spoiled the lass[8].'

It is important to note that this Eliza is not the one later remembered in Elizabeth Branwell's will, but a more distant relation as John Branwell Williams was the son of another John Williams and Alice Branwell, sister of Thomas Branwell, Elizabeth and Maria's father. It is interesting, however, that this Eliza is interested in botany, as this is also something that became associated with another distant relative from Cornwall: Elizabeth Carne.

Elizabeth Carne was born in 1817 to Joseph Carne, whose father William Carne shared a grandfather with the Brontë's own grandmother Anne Carne Branwell[9]. Elizabeth Carne was one of the nineteenth century's great renaissance women, the author of a number of books, she also served as head of the Batten, Carne and Oxnam Bank, and she became one of the leading naturalists and geologists of her day. It's interesting to note that her first book, *Three Months Rest at Pau in the Winter and Spring of 1859*, was written under the male pseudonym of John Altrayd Wittitterly; perhaps taking the idea from her distant cousins in Yorkshire.

If Thomas Brontë Branwell had made his trip from Cornwall to Haworth in 1851 with romance in mind, he was given short shrift, but he married Sarah Hannah Jones a year later. In 1854, Charlotte did something that none of her siblings, her aunt Elizabeth, or her great friends Ellen Nussey and Mary Taylor ever did; she married. In the preceding years she had mingled in exalted company, mixing with the likes of William Makepeace Thackeray, Elizabeth Gaskell, Harriet Martineau and Sir James and Lady Kay Shuttleworth, but her husband was found a little closer to home.

Arthur Bell Nicholls, originally from County Antrim, had been assistant curate to Patrick Brontë since May 1845. He provided exemplary service to the family, including conducting Emily's funeral[10], but they seemed to be oblivious to his growing attachment to one of their number, and when he finally proposed to Charlotte he was given a very frosty reception, with the father furious and daughter bewildered. Feeling he had made a fool of himself Arthur announced that he was leaving Haworth for life as a missionary in Australia. His last sermon saw him shaking in the pulpit unable to speak, until he was helped out of the church by his parishioners. Charlotte wrote to Ellen of what she expected to be her last meeting with him:

'He left Haworth this morning at 6' o clock... He went out thinking he was not to see me – And indeed until the very last moment – I thought it best not. But perceiving that he stayed long before going out at the gate – and remembering his long grief I took courage and went out trembling and miserable. I found him leaning again the garden-door in a paroxysm of anguish – sobbing as women never sob[11].'

Galvanised by this meeting, Arthur left not for Australia but Kirk Smeaton near Pontefract, from where he continued to correspond with Charlotte. He returned to Haworth on 29 June 1854 to wed her; Charlotte soon realised, against all her expectations, that she had fallen in love with her new husband. It was a happy but all too brief marriage. Charlotte fell pregnant, but suffered from the excessive morning sickness, hyperemesis gravidurum. Unable to eat or drink, she wasted slowly away, dying in her new husband's arms on 31 March 1855.

The Brontë line was over, and Patrick had the sad fate of outliving his wife and all six of his children. There are Brontës today who are descended from Patrick's siblings and cousins in Ireland who, following his lead, adopted the spelling of Brontë rather than Brunty. What, however, became of the Branwell line? It is the Branwell influence rather than the Brontë influence, after all, that can be seen most clearly in the works of Charlotte, Emily and Anne, thanks to their upbringing at the hands of their Aunt Elizabeth. This line of the family becomes even more important if we accept the opinion given by J. Hambley Rowe, chair of the Brontë Society Council, in 1923:

'While much has been written and more conjectured regarding the ancestry of the Brontës on the paternal side, their maternal forebears have been uniformly neglected. This seems the more inexplicable as it is generally considered that the distaff influences are the more important in the moulding of capabilities and temperament[12].'

Out of Thomas and Anne Branwell's offspring, born between 1769 and 1789, only four had children, and many of those children in turn died young or unmarried. This is most noticeable in the family of Benjamin Branwell, one-time mayor of Penzance and the only brother of Elizabeth to survive into adulthood. He and his wife Mary had five daughters and three sons, not one of whom married. His son Thomas grew into adulthood and served as a solicitor, and three of his daughters ran their own school except for the reclusive Lydia who preferred a solitary life.

The family of Charlotte Branwell and her cousin Joseph endured longer, even though out of their ten children, only Thomas Brontë Branwell, the visitor to Haworth, married. Thomas and his wife Sarah, in turn, had but one child who married; Arthur Milton Cooper Branwell who, keeping up the family tradition, married a cousin in 1897. She was Charlotte Brontë Jones, daughter of a brother to Thomas Brontë Branwell's wife Sarah Hannah Jones. With forenames of Charlotte Brontë it is perhaps fitting that Miss Jones married the son of a cousin of the original Charlotte Brontë.

Arthur Branwell became a captain in the British army, and he and Charlotte had one son, christened Patrick Arthur Brontë Branwell, born in 1904. At the time of his mother Charlotte's death in 1942 he was the sole surviving descendent of Thomas and Anne Branwell alive in England. An interesting story regarding Charlotte Branwell's will appeared in a Leeds newspaper shortly afterwards, under the headline 'Brontë Relics and Will Lost in Raid':

> 'Charlotte Brontë relics were mentioned to Mr. Justice Langton in the probate court in London to-day. The judge granted probate of the copy of the late Mrs. Charlotte Brontë Branwell, of Brompton Road, London, to her only son, Patrick Arthur Brontë Branwell, the sole surviving devisee and legatee... Mrs. Branwell left to the Brontë Museum (if her son predeceased her) the Branwell miniatures, a picture of Miss Branwell (who sent the Brontë sisters to Brussels), a picture painted by Charlotte Brontë, four pictures worked in silk by the aunts of Charlotte Brontë, a workbox which belonged to Charlotte Brontë, and a letter signed by Mr. C. Brontë framed in oak. The son of Mrs. Branwell did not predecease his mother. Mrs. Branwell's will fell to ashes after being taken from the strongroom of her solicitor after an air raid, but the solicitor had copies of all the wills in their charge deposited at their bankers[13].'

Patrick Branwell did not marry Anthea Mary Hunt until he was 53, and when he died in 1964 the Branwell family line that had produced the Brontës came to an end in England. That does not mean that the Branwell story came to an end. Jane and Eliza Kingston, remembered alongside Charlotte, Emily and Anne in Elizabeth Branwell's will, had fascinating and tragic lives that could have come from a Brontë novel, yet it is thanks to Jane, the prototype of Helen Graham, that there are Branwell descendants thriving today on another continent.

Chapter 17

Going on a Voyage

'One day, nearly seven years ago, a Mr. Eyre came to Gateshead and wanted to see you; Missis said you were at school fifty miles off; he seemed so much disappointed, for he could not stay: he was going on a voyage to a foreign country, and the ship was to sail from London in a day or two.'

Charlotte Brontë, *Jane Eyre*

When Elizabeth Branwell made her will in April 1833, it was only natural that she made provision for the three girls she was raising as if they were her own children, but she also left an equal share to Elizabeth Jane Kingston in Penzance. Nothing was left to her other nephews and nieces, the sons and daughters of her brother Benjamin and her sister Charlotte, so why did she single out Elizabeth Jane, henceforth referred to as Eliza, in this way? The answer reveals a lot about Elizabeth Branwell's character, and it also opens up one of the most heartbreaking stories in the Branwell-Brontë family history.

As with her nephew Branwell, Elizabeth expected that the children of Benjamin and Charlotte would have little need of financial assistance in their adult lives, so she instead concentrated on helping the most obviously needy in the form of her sister Jane and her daughter Eliza.

Jane Branwell, as we have seen, married the celebrated Wesleyan preacher John Kingston in Penzance in June 1800, but by 1807 he had been dismissed from the Wesleyan movement in disgrace, and he, his pregnant wife Jane and their four children left for a new life in the new world of America.

The nature of John's offence remains a mystery, but there are tantalising clues. In his memoirs published in *The Methodist Magazine* in the year prior to his marriage, Kingston talks of weaknesses in his character, and hints at having led a dissolute life before being struck by a religious conversion:

'My parents, who lived at Towcester in Northamptonshire (the place of my nativity) were greatly alarmed when they heard of the change which had commenced in my life and conversation, till I assured them, that I had only forsaken the mad and frantic ways of an evil world ... After a season, I began to discover the root of inbred sin, which brought me into various trials and distresses. My natural flow of spirits exposed me to manifold temptations, but band-meetings ... helped me to break thro' the snares of the wicked one[1].'

By 1797, as he prepares to return to England from the West Indies, he is still battling his demons:

'I found great cause for gratitude to my heavenly benefactor ... but at the same time I felt the great need of purity of heart, and groaned for deliverance from pride and evil tempers. And altho' my desires were engaged to serve the Lord above all things, yet I found many hindrances; difficulties, and dangers were before me, being surrounded by war, and many temptations within and without[2].'

Temptations were certainly the downfall of John Kingston, but of what particular nature did they take? In 1807 he was tried by his peers and then dismissed summarily, losing both his reputation and his livelihood. An offence leading to this sentence, rather than an admonishment or suspension, must have been serious, but the nature of it remained unspecified[3], so we are left wondering if he had misappropriated monies, or been guilty of offences particularly frowned upon by the Wesleyan church such as marital infidelity or drunkenness.

His daughter Eliza later wrote that her father 'was a man of strong passions, and had, no doubt, great temptations[4].'

Eliza's opinion of John Kingston must have been based upon the recollections of her mother Jane, as they took their leave of him when she was less than a year old. It was a sad, rather pathetic farewell, as mother and baby separated from father and three children. John was left with just one treasured memento of his daughter Eliza; a slip of paper containing a cutting of her hair, upon which he wrote:

'Hair from the head of my little daughter Eliz. Jane 10 months old who left me this morning with her mother for New York in order to embark for old England. J. Kingston, April 25th, 1809[5].'

Upon their arrival in Baltimore a year earlier, John Kingston and his family took up residence at 25, Market Street, which as well as being a living place he turned into a book shop and publishing house. It was a precarious industry, and far removed from the life of a respected preacher he had enjoyed when he last entered the city in October 1795. The climate and lifestyle of Baltimore were particularly alien to his wife Jane who had never left England before, and she must have endured terrible hardships to make her turn her back on her husband and four eldest children; we can only assume that John Kingston's temptations had returned.

John Kingston was both a bookseller and a book publisher in America, but he was also a book writer and, at first, a successful one. His pocket biographical dictionary rapidly sold out of its initial run of 1,500 copies[6], leading him to create a second edition in 1811, 'improved' and 'embellished with portraits'. This book reveals a learned man with a huge breadth of knowledge, but it may also give us a clue as to the demons he faced.

The biographical dictionary deals with figures throughout history, so that we see three pages dedicated to the Caesars of Rome, for example. A figure largely forgotten today, however, gets fifteen pages; the Swiss philosopher and scientist Johann Georg Zimmermann. His entry discusses his time as court physician to George III of England, and also his writing of his hugely successful (at the time) book *Solitude*. There is also an extended and rather odd passage that details Zimmermann's struggles against a secret order known as the Illuminated, with a dire warning that:

> 'To destroy the Christian religion, and to overthrow every throne, and every government, has been from the year 1776, the constant aim of the Secret Order of the Illuminated[7].'

Zimmermann suffered increasingly from 'disorder' which rendered him incapable of any action, from eating to sleeping, and his life is summed up thus:

> 'Zimmerman, on the whole, was very amiable in his private manners: and at times he was cheerful, even to gaiety. But the afflictions of Europe were his... There are those who have felt with Zimmerman; and like him have fallen! Many excellent men – men whose wisdom was high, but unassuming, and grounded too on the basis of piety, have sunk under the increasing pressure of this dark and distorted day[8].'

Was John Kingston's high regard of Zimmermann because he himself was one of those pious men who had fallen and sunk under the pressure of a dark and distorted day? It could be that, for all the charges whispered against him down the centuries, John Kingston's real crime was that he suffered from what we would today recognise as a depressive disorder or a mental psychosis.

The Kingston book business soon foundered, and John was left with little money to raise his four children. In 1818, he returned briefly to London to visit his sister there, in the hope of raising funds for a new business venture. She was unable or unwilling to help, but John must also have informed his estranged wife of his journey to England – probably with the hope of obtaining some Branwell family money – for she travelled to London to see not him, but her children. It was nine years since she had last laid eyes upon them and she was shocked by what she saw; they were impoverished and half-starved, and Jane begged John to allow her to take them back to Penzance with her. He refused, and they returned with him to Baltimore[9].

It was a bleak return, and Jane's firstborn daughter, named Maria after her sister, died of fever shortly after arriving back in Baltimore. Sometime in 1823 or 1824, John Kingston made a last desperate move to New York city, but his slide into complete and utter poverty continued and he died of pleurisy in April 1824[10]. This sad end to a once-celebrated life led to the fragmentation of his family. His son, also named John Kingston, like many others of this time headed to new territories in the west of America, but as there are no records of him after this point it is likely to have been an unsuccessful, and short, endeavour. Thomas returned to London to live initially with the aunt he had met in 1818, but he too descended into poverty before dying in 1855. Middle daughter Anne Branwell Kingston remained in New York earning a living as a seamstress, where her fortunes improved as in 1830 she married a man from a well-respected German Pennsylvanian family called Joseph Bergstresser, who was on the verge of becoming a successful businessman. Anne's happiness was short lived, for in 1835 she died of a fever leaving behind two young children.

The tale of the Kingstons in America then seems to be a tragic one, but the Kingstons of Penzance were protected, at least at first, by the financial support of Elizabeth Branwell. Her will, written in 1833, refers to 'having advanced to my sister Kingston the sum of twenty-five pounds[11]', and this payment helped Jane and Eliza turn their home at 10, Morrab Place into a guest house. It was at this address that they received a letter from Joseph Burgster (like the Bruntys and Brontës and the Bramwells and Branwells, he had changed the spelling of his name) informing Jane and Eliza of the death of their daughter and sister. Jane wrote back offering to take his children, Maria and Joseph junior, and raise them in Penzance, but Joseph instead took them with him back to Pennsylvania.

This correspondence went cold for nearly two decades but in 1854, for reasons unknown, Joseph wrote again to his sister-in-law Eliza in Penzance, and the letters that then flowed between them reveals a tale of pathos and sadness.

Eliza was still living with her mother Jane, by this time 81, but the guest house was not paying their way; it was the annuity from Thomas Branwell and the legacy from Elizabeth that allowed them to lead relatively comfortable lives. Eliza gave a description of herself to Joseph Burgster, and her self-deprecating frankness is very redolent of her cousin Charlotte Brontë:

> 'My dear Brother, you ask me do I look like Anne. Alas, no! I fear I am neither like her in features, form, or disposition. My mother thinks she was her best child, and I am about the worst, but you shall judge for yourself. I am of middle stature, rather large boned, but not very fleshy, high shouldered, short necked, neither fair nor dark, high cheek bones, large mouth, irregular teeth, grey eyes, brown hair, *very* grey on the front part of my head... of an irritable temper, but frank and open with those I like, rather impudently so sometimes. To crown all, I am an *Old Maid of 46*, or shall be so on the 23rd of this month[12].'

Elizabeth Branwell's sister Jane died the year after this letter was sent, 1855, but the cross-Atlantic correspondence between Eliza and Joseph continued. From these letters we learn that Eliza Kingston knew of the literary success of her cousins, and co-legatees of their aunt's will, the Brontës, and had read their books:

> 'A cousin of mine who was known in the literary world by the name of Currer Bell, the author of "Jane Eyre" has written three or four very interesting and original works. Did you see them[13]?'

In another letter, however, Eliza was rather less complimentary about her cousin Emily's only novel:

'I wish my cousin had never written "Wuthering Heights," although it is considered clever by some[14].'

This letter from Eliza to Joseph, dating from March 1860, also reveals that there continued to be correspondence between Haworth and Penzance. Patrick Brontë, by then aged 82 and having lost all his family members, had sent his niece Eliza a letter:

'I had a letter from my Uncle Brontë last June. He says he was in his 83rd year, but, though feeble, was still able to preach once on Sunday, and sometimes to take occasional duty; his son-in-law, Mr. Nicholls will continue with him. He says strangers still continue to call, but he converses little with them, but keeps himself as quiet as he can. I understand the Brontës were beloved in their own neighbourhood[15].'

It is thanks to Eliza Kingston that we get this final glimpse into the life of the man who died in June 1861, the last of the Brontës. Evidently his love of Maria Branwell and his fond memories of Elizabeth Branwell made it a pleasure for him to continue a correspondence with their relative in Cornwall.

Eliza invested the money she received from her mother's will, saved from Jane's £50 a year annuity, and the money she had left from her Aunt Elizabeth's will, in shares in Cornish tin and copper mines. They prospered well initially, but soon the market collapsed with devastating effect and through her letters to Joseph we see her following the same path as her father and siblings: a descent into poverty.

By 1871, she was no longer running the guest house, but was instead a 'librarian and tea dealer' living in South Parade, Penzance[16]. These endeavours too foundered, and she writes of how she can no longer afford to attend the choral society or theatre, as she had once loved to do. Finally, she writes of having to sell her final mining share for £10 that she had once bought for £105, and is later reduced to writing begging letters to charities and wealthy individuals:

'I thought some time since that there are institutions for the help of those in reduced circumstances, I would try to ascertain their rules. One, the National Benevolent Institution, does not help those under 60. I am not yet 58. I was advised to write Miss Burdett Coutts who is said to be the richest commoner in the United Kingdom. I did it on the 1ˢᵗ of this month... but received no reply, the case twice before to others[17].'

There is one further, terrible yet touching, letter from Eliza that lays bare with characteristic frankness the degradation she had now reached:

> 'I feel very weak at times, if I over-exert myself or do not take sufficient nourishment; I require (if I could have it) animal food every day ... I cannot live so low as I used to. I was informed that it was a case of nervous debility which I knew before ... there is often a cobweb (or something like it) floating before my left eye ... I live in constant dread of the future ... I have no prospect of a home or rooms or indeed any money to pay rent ... God only knows how it will end ... I sometimes feel as if my heart would break[18].'

Eliza valued greatly her correspondence with Joseph; he had become her only friend, but was too far away to help. Although in one reply he offered her a chance to live with him and his family in America, she could not bear the thought of travelling to the country of her birth. Eventually, no longer able to afford stamps, the flow of letters from Eliza was brought to a halt. She now endured a fate eerily similar to the father she had never known. Eliza's complete destitution brought on a physical and mental collapse, and she died in a ward for the mentally ill at the Union Hospital in Madron in 1878[19].

Fourteen years after Eliza's death, Amelia Josephina Branwell, daughter of Benjamin and Mary, died aged 76, the last of the Brontës' Cornish cousins. This was not, however, the end of the Branwell line started by Thomas and his wife Anne. Joseph Burgster's wife Anne, originally Anne Kingston and the daughter of John and Jane Kingston, nee Branwell, died aged 32, but she left a daughter Maria Louisa Burgster and a son Joseph Kingston Burgster. Maria married Jacob Horning and Joseph married Hattie Goodell. Joseph's line ended in the following generation, but it's a different story for the children of Maria and Jacob. Unlike the Branwells of Penzance these Branwell descendants in America prospered, and their line continues to this day.

As I write this, there are at least eight such people across America, in Texas, California and Missouri. They have remarkable tales of their own, including among them a Vietnam war veteran and a leading pathologist, but as their ancestor Emily Brontë craved, their anonymity will be preserved. Nevertheless, these first cousins of the Brontës several times removed are the closest living relatives of Charlotte, Emily and Anne Brontë in the world today.

The Branwell family that gave us Elizabeth and Maria, and through her the Brontë siblings, was and is a fascinating one, but there is one further interesting point raised by a woman who remembered Eliza Kingston, a Mrs Breffitt who was the daughter of one of Elizabeth Branwell's cousins:

> 'I think my mother asked Miss [Eliza] Kingston about Charlotte Brontë on more than one occasion. They talked about her together, and Miss Kingston spoke a good deal about what Charlotte Brontë had brought out in her works, and how she depicted characters. I have a vivid recollection of wonder that our poor cousin Eliza Jane could say such beautiful things and see so much in books, and yet look so plain and prosper so badly. Is there any record of the book she wrote, or was it only a part? Perhaps she destroyed it. She said no one would publish it[20].'

We now see that all four of the nieces that Elizabeth Branwell supported equally in her will, Charlotte, Emily, Anne and Eliza, used the freedom the legacy gave them to write books; there, sadly, the similarity ended.

Chapter 18

A Mother's Care

'Our children, Edward, Agnes, and little Mary, promise well; their education, for the time being, is chiefly committed to me; and they shall want for no good thing that a mother's care can give. Our modest income is amply sufficient for our requirements: and by practising the economy we learnt in harder times, and never attempting to imitate our richer neighbours, we manage not only to enjoy comfort and contentment ourselves, but to have every year something to lay by for our children, and something to give to those who need it. And now I think I have said sufficient.'

Anne Brontë, *Agnes Grey*

It is more than 175 years since the death of Elizabeth Branwell, and only now are people realising the contribution she made to the lives of the Brontës and the magnificent works they produced, and only now are people looking beyond the misconceptions that some have held of her.

Early biographers of the Brontë sisters created a perverse distortion of Elizabeth's role, blaming her for the gloom that often descended upon the lives of the siblings within Haworth Parsonage. This is far from the truth, and is based mainly upon the testimony of the servant Martha Wright and the opinions of Charlotte Brontë.

Charlotte was never her aunt's favourite, and for that reason Elizabeth was never a favourite of hers. Charlotte Brontë was a woman who always spoke her mind and could, at times, be scathing even of those she loved, as when she wrote to Ellen Nussey that she had confronted Margaret Wooler and:

'I told her one or two rather plain truths - which set her a crying ... I should have respected her far more if she had turned me out of doors instead of crying for two days and two nights together – I was in a regular passion my "warm temper" quite got the better of me – Of which I don't boast for it was a weakness – nor am I ashamed of it[1].'

Miss Wooler became one of Charlotte's best friends, so we can see from this that she wasn't averse to giving a sharp opinion of someone when she thought they deserved it. It may be such forthright opinions that led Elizabeth Gaskell to write that:

> 'The children respected her [Elizabeth Branwell], and had that sort of affection which is generated by esteem; but I do not think they ever freely loved her[2].'

The two Elizabeths, Gaskell and Branwell, never met, and so the opinion given above is based primarily upon Charlotte's recollections; while this respect, but not love, may well reflect her feelings, it is certainly not true of others who came to know her, such as Anne and Branwell Brontë.

Another accusation still, on occasion, levelled against Elizabeth Branwell is that she was a severe Methodist who looked down upon fun and trivialities in general. This view of Elizabeth comes from Martha Wright and from Mary Taylor, who as we have seen took umbrage at being scolded for using the word 'spitting.' Martha Wright had other axes to grind after being summarily dismissed from service at the parsonage not long after Elizabeth's arrival. It may be that Martha had taken too much of a liking to the ale that was kept in the parsonage cellar, for Elizabeth insisted on having the cellar key and carefully rationed how much ale each servant was allowed to have on a daily basis. This was a sensible economy, and it should be noted that Elizabeth did not ban the consumption of alcohol altogether despite her Wesleyan beliefs.

Tabitha Brown was also less-than-enamoured of Elizabeth, reporting that:

> 'You know Miss Branwell was a real, old tyke. She made the girls work at their sewing, and what with their father's strictness over their lessons, and the hours they devoted to needlework, they had little time for themselves until after nine o'clock at night, and that was when they got time for their writing[3].'

Tabitha was the sister of Martha Brown, who didn't enter service at the parsonage until December 1839, when the Brontë girls were aged between

19 and 23 and no longer in the habit of taking lessons or sewing instruction. Her second-hand testimony of a strict childhood regime is also contradicted by Emily and Anne's diary paper of 1834, when we see the teenage girls 'pitter-pottering' in the middle of the day, not yet having done their homework.

Even Charlotte rides to the defence of her aunt's reputation, as her letters show how much she loved the parsonage home that Elizabeth had control over, and whilst she never once states that her aunt was stern or unkind, in 1841 she wrote that: 'Aunt is in high good humour[4].'

One further accusation against Elizabeth is that she tried to have Tabby Ayckroyd removed from the parsonage at a time that she needed the Brontës' support. Tabby broke her leg in the winter of 1836, after slipping on ice; it was a bad injury, and left her unable to do the household duties she was employed to carry out. Elizabeth did suggest that it would be better for Tabby to leave their employ, but her reasons for this have not been examined. Undoubtedly Elizabeth had one eye on the ever-precarious finances of the parsonage, but she may also have thought Tabby would receive better care being looked after by her sister Susannah. The children, who loved Tabby dearly, were having none of it and threatened to go on hunger strike unless it was agreed that she could stay. Elizabeth then consented to Tabby remaining at the parsonage[5], which in itself is testimony to her flexibility and her compassion.

Perhaps the most unfair of all the accusations against Elizabeth Branwell is that she was a religious zealot whose hellfire version of Christianity depressed her niece Anne so much that it led to her breakdown at Roe Head and blighted the lives of all the siblings. This is far removed from the truth. Elizabeth's views differed greatly from those of the Calvinists; as a Wesleyan she believed in a loving God and a fairer society. We also know that neither she nor her family were overly rigid when it came to Wesleyan doctrine, as we hear of Elizabeth taking snuff and enjoying music and dances, whilst her family went as far as owning inns and breweries.

Elizabeth taught her nephew and nieces to study the Bible as part of their education, and she was undoubtedly a religious woman herself, but she did not force her beliefs upon others, as we can see from her continued support of, and love for, Emily and Branwell even after they stopped attending church. It was Calvinist preaching that oppressed Anne, especially in her youth, but this was far removed from the teaching and beliefs of her aunt.

Branwell's praise of his aunt after her death is the most powerful defence of all. She was much more than simply a woman who had come from

Cornwall to run the household and keep her sister's children in check; she was as a mother to him. Even more than this, she was not a woman who stopped them having fun, or that simply looked on as they had fun, she was the instigator of the fun, the woman who was at the centre of all his happy childhood days.

Let us draw back the dark curtains that some have enveloped her in, and see Elizabeth Branwell for what she really was: an immensely kind woman, a clever and educated woman, a loving woman who was fulsome in both her emotional and financial support, and a woman who always put her family before herself up to her very last day.

Aunt Branwell created not a four-walled prison at the parsonage, but an environment in which individuality was indulged and creativity allowed to flourish. From the mittens she knitted for Ellen Nussey, to the books she bought for the Brontë children, she could be relied upon to know what would be truly useful, and to supply it. Above all else, Elizabeth was a woman who could be relied upon and to children who had lost their mother at such tender ages, there was nothing more important.

Even in death the money she had accumulated by going without the things she loved herself, made a huge and positive difference to the lives of the four nieces she left it to. The years 2016 to 2020 mark a four-year period encompassing the 200th anniversaries of the births of Charlotte, Branwell, Emily and Anne Brontë; dates that are rightly being celebrated at the Brontë Parsonage Museum and across the world. It would be fitting if similar celebrations were held in 2026 to mark the 250th birthday of Elizabeth Branwell; after all, not only was she a fine human being who gave up all she knew and loved to help her sister and then her children, but it is certain that without her there would be none of the Brontë books that we treasure today. It's time to give Elizabeth Branwell the central place within the Brontë story that her actions deserve.

Notes

Preface

1. Letter from Branwell Brontë to Francis Grundy, 29 October 1842.

Chapter 1

1. Gaskell, Elizabeth, *The Life Of Charlotte Brontë*, p. 96
2. Thornhill, Richard, *Wuthering Heights and the Fairy Cave, Northern Earth 90*, p. 17
3. Brontë, Emily, *Wuthering Heights*, p. 161
4. du Maurier, Daphne, *Vanishing Cornwall*, p. 13
5. Drew, Samuel and Hitchens, Fortescue, *The History of Cornwall from the Earliest Records & Traditions, to the Present Time, Volume I*, p. 98
6. 'The Philosopher' by Emily Brontë, ms. Brontë Parsonage Museum, Haworth
7. Sagar-Fenton, Mike, *Penzance: The Biography*, p. 17

Chapter 2

1. Orel, Harold [Ed.], *The Brontës: Interviews And Recollections*, p. 25
2. Hardie-Budden, Melissa, *Penzance 2000*, p. 18
3. Carter, Clive, *The Port of Penzance – A History*, pp. 6-7
4. Carpenter, Stanley D.M., *The English Civil War*, p. 493
5. Besley, Henry, *The Route Book of Cornwall*, p. 111
6. Defoe, Daniel, *A Tour Thro' the Whole Island of Great Britain, by a Gentleman*, p. 350
7. Rowe, J. Hambley, 'The Maternal Relatives of the Brontës', *Brontë Society Transactions 1923, Volume 6, Issue 33*, p. 135
8. Will of Thomas Branwell, Merchant of Penzance, Cornwall, Proved in the Court of Exeter, now at National Archives, Kew, London
9. Barker, Juliet, *The Brontës*, p. 49

Chapter 3

1. Some of James Tonkin's work can be seen at Penlee House, the stately Penzance home built in 1865 for John Richards Branwell and now a museum and art gallery.

2. Edgerley, C. Mabel, *'Elizabeth Branwell – The "Small, Antiquated Lady"'*, Brontë Society Transactions 1937, Volume 9, Issue 2, p. 104
3. Will of Thomas Branwell, Merchant of Penzance, Cornwall, Proved in the Court of Exeter, now at National Archives, Kew, London
4. Brontë, Anne, *Agnes Grey*, p. 3
5. Newbold, Margaret, *'The Branwell Saga'*, Brontë Studies 2002, Volume 27, Issue 1, p. 19
6. Dickinson, H.T. [ed.], *A Companion to Eighteenth-Century Britain*, p. 190
7. As revealed in the 1850 General Board of Health inspection undertaken by Benjamin Herschel Babbage.
8. Schwartz, Maurice [ed.], *Encyclopedia of Coastal Science*, p. 1018
9. *Leeds Mercury*, 11th September 1824
10. du Maurier, Daphne, *Vanishing Cornwall*, p. 53

Chapter 4

1. Leifchild, J.R., *Cornwall, Its Mines and Miners*, p. 36
2. Barker, Juliet, *The Brontës*, p. 49
3. Carter, Clive, *The Port of Penzance – A History*, p. 8
4. Lloyd, Frederick, *An Accurate and Impartial Life of the Late Lord Viscount Nelson*, pp. 149-50
5. *Daily Mail*, 27 February 2008
6. Edgerley, C. Mabel, *'Elizabeth Branwell – The "Small, Antiquated Lady"'*, Brontë Society Transactions 1937, Volume 9, Issue 2, p. 104
7. Green, Dudley, *Patrick Brontë – Father of Genius*, p. 111
8. Holgate, Ivy, *'The Branwells at Penzance'*, Brontë Studies 1960, Volume 5, p. 431
9. Brontë, Charlotte, *Shirley*, p. 296
10. Newbold, Margaret, *'The Branwell Saga'*, Brontë Studies 2002, Volume 27, Issue 1, p. 19
11. Ibid.
12. Austen, Jane, *Northanger Abbey*, p. 23
13. Hardie-Budden, Melissa, *'Maternal Forebears of the Brontë Archive: 'Nothing Comes from Nothing'; or Stories from Another Canon'*, Brontë Studies 2015, Volume 40, Issue 4, p. 271
14. Carne, John, *Letters From the East*, p. 426

Chapter 5

1. Barker, Juliet, *The Brontës*, p. 49
2. Ibid.
3. Barnard, Louise and Barnard, Robert, *A Brontë Encyclopedia*, p. 108
4. Hardie-Budden, Melissa, *'Maternal Forebears of the Brontë Archive: 'Nothing Comes from Nothing'; or Stories from Another Canon'*, Brontë Studies 2015, Volume 40, Issue 4, p. 273
5. Hardie-Budden, Melissa, *Penzance 2000*, p. 64
6. Wesley, John, *The Heart of John Wesley's Journal*, p. 299

7. Dobree, Bonamy, *John Wesley*, p. 80
8. Greenwood, Robin, *West Lane and Hall Green Baptist Churches in Haworth in West Yorkshire, their Early History and Doctrinal Distinctives*, p. 93
9. Warren, Samuel, *Chronicles of Wesleyan Methodism*, p. 168
10. Kingston, Rev. John, '*Memoirs of the Life of John Kingston, Preacher of the Gospel*', *The Methodist Magazine for the Year 1799, Volume XXII*, p. 209
11. Kingston, Rev. John, '*Memoirs of the Life of John Kingston, Preacher of the Gospel*', *The Methodist Magazine for the Year 1799, Volume XXII*, p. 210
12. Kingston, Rev. John, '*Memoirs of the Life of John Kingston, Preacher of the Gospel*', *The Methodist Magazine for the Year 1799, Volume XXII*, p. 262
13. Warren, Samuel, *Chronicles of Wesleyan Methodism*, p. 93
14. Elizabeth is also recorded as a witness at her sister Jane's wedding, along with Thomas Longley, another Wesleyan preacher.
15. Davy, John, *Memoirs of the Life of Sir Humphry Davy*, pp. 10-11
16. Edgerley, C. Mabel, '*Elizabeth Branwell – The "Small, Antiquated Lady"*', *Brontë Society Transactions 1937, Volume 9, Issue 2*, p. 105

Chapter 6

1. Colenso, William, *Ancient and Modern History of Mount's Bay*, p. 56
2. Colenso, William, *Ancient and Modern History of Mount's Bay*, p. 57
3. Warren, Samuel, *Chronicles of Wesleyan Methodism*, p. 217
4. Warren, Samuel, *Chronicles of Wesleyan Methodism*, p. 196
5. The other witness in the parish register of St Maddern's church on this occasion was father of the bride, John Batten.
6. The list of Mayors of Penzance is at the Cornwall Record Office, Truro.
7. See chapter 17.
8. Kingston, Rev. John, '*Memoirs of the Life of John Kingston, Preacher of the Gospel*', *The Methodist Magazine for the Year 1799 Volume XXII*, p. 264
9. Will of Thomas Branwell, Merchant of Penzance, Cornwall, Proved in the Court of Exeter, now at National Archives, Kew, London
10. See measuringworth.com for further explanations of the calculations giving £50 in 1808 a current labour value of £42,940, an economic status value of £48,810 and an economic power value of £250,000.
11. Newbold, Margaret, '*The Branwell Saga*', *Brontë Studies 2002, Volume 27, Issue 1*, p. 20
12. Holgate, Ivy, '*The Branwells at Penzance*', *Brontë Studies 1960, Volume 5*, p. 431
13. This son, Richard Branwell Veale, was acknowledged and remembered in his father's will.
14. Clarke, James Stanier [Ed.], *The Naval Chronicle: Volume 27, January-July 1812*, p. 45
15. Scruton, William, *Thornton and the Brontës*, pp. 69-70
16. Green, Dudley, *Patrick Brontë: Father of Genius*, pp. 25-6
17. The manuscript of Maria Branwell's '*The Advantages of Poverty in Religious Concerns*', lovingly preserved by Patrick Brontë, is now in the Brotherton Library archives, Leeds.

18. Green, Dudley, *Patrick Brontë: Father of Genius*, p. 63
19. Chadwick, Ellis H., *In the Footsteps of the Brontës*, p. 36
20. *The Cornish Telegraph*, 25 December 1884

Chapter 7

1. Barker, Juliet, *The Brontës*, p. 51
2. Newbold, Margaret, *'The Branwell Saga'*, *Brontë Studies 2002, Volume 27, Issue 1*, p. 22
3. Newbold, Margaret, *'The Branwell Saga'*, *Brontë Studies 2002, Volume 27, Issue 1*, p. 23
4. Letter from Charlotte Brontë to Constantin Heger, 24 July 1844, ms. British Library, London
5. Green, Dudley, *Patrick Brontë: Father of Genius*, p. 67
6. Yates, William Walsh, *The Father of the Brontës*, pp. 91-2
7. Brontë, Charlotte, *Shirley*, p. 361
8. Barker, Juliet, *The Brontës*, p. 61
9. Edgerley, C. Mabel, *'Elizabeth Branwell – The "Small, Antiquated Lady"'*, *Brontë Society Transactions 1937, Volume 9, Issue 2*, p. 106
10. Gaskell, Elizabeth, *The Life Of Charlotte Brontë*, p. 82
11. Whilst the book would have a considerable value simply for belonging to Maria Branwell, its huge price was thanks to two previously unseen stories in tiny script hidden within the book written by a young Charlotte Brontë.
12. According to the public information board in Thornton, supplied by Bradford council.
13. Letter from Patrick Brontë to Richard Burn, 27 January 1820, ms. Brontë Parsonage Museum, Haworth
14. Diary of Elizabeth Firth, ms. Sheffield University Library
15. Ibid.
16. Ibid.
17. Ibid.
18. Edgerley, C. Mabel, *'Elizabeth Branwell – The "Small, Antiquated Lady"'*, *Brontë Society Transactions 1937, Volume 9, Issue 2*, p. 106

Chapter 8

1. Green, Dudley, *Patrick Brontë – Father of Genius*, p. 77
2. *Leeds Intelligencer*, 14 June 1819
3. Archbishop Longley letters archive, Lambeth Palace, London
4. Ratchford, Fannie E., *'The Loneliness of a Brontë Cousin'*, *Brontë Society Transactions 1957, Volume 13, Issue 2*, p. 105
5. The letter, unfortunately, no longer exists, but we know Patrick must have sent it, and the contents within it, from Elizabeth Branwell's subsequent actions. We also know that Patrick continued to write to the Branwells in Penzance throughout his life, as Eliza Kingston wrote that she had received a letter from him in 1860.
6. Green, Dudley [Ed.], *The Letters Of The Reverend Patrick Brontë*, p. 43

7. Dinsdale, Ann, *'Mrs Brontë's Nurse'*, *Brontë Studies 2005, Volume 30, Issue 3*, p. 258
8. Barker, Juliet, *The Brontës*, p. 102
9. Rhodes, Professor Philip, *'A Medical Appraisal of the Brontës'*, *Brontë Society Transactions 1972, Volume 16, Issue 2*, p. 102
10. Gaskell, Elizabeth, *The Life Of Charlotte Brontë*, p. 87
11. Orel, Harold [Ed.], *The Brontës: Interviews And Recollections*, p. 143
12. Green, Dudley [Ed.], *The Letters Of The Reverend Patrick Brontë*, p. 43

Chapter 9

1. Barnard, Louise and Barnard, Robert, *A Brontë Encyclopedia*, pp. 110-1
2. Barker, Juliet, *The Brontës*, p. 102
3. Barker, Juliet, *The Brontës*, p. 103
4. Shorter, Clement, *The Brontës and Their Circle*, p. 38
5. Letter from Isabella Dury to Miss Mariner, 14 February 1823, ms. Brontë Parsonage Museum, Haworth
6. Diary of Elizabeth Firth, ms. Sheffield University Library
7. Orel, Harold [Ed.], *The Brontës: Interviews And Recollections*, p. 25
8. *Scribner's Monthly*, vol. II, issue 1, May 1871
9. Chadwick, Ellis H., *In the Footsteps of the Brontës*, p. 69
10. Letter from Patrick Brontë to Richard Burns, 25 August 1825
11. Barker, Juliet, *The Brontës*, p. 105
12. Green, Dudley [Ed.], *The Letters Of The Reverend Patrick Brontë*, p. 44
13. Edgerley, C. Mabel, *'Elizabeth Branwell – The "Small, Antiquated Lady"'*, *Brontë Society Transactions 1937, Volume 9, Issue 2*, p. 107
14. Green, Dudley [Ed.], *The Letters Of The Reverend Patrick Brontë*, p. 54
15. *The Journal Of Education, January 1900*, ms. British Library, London
16. Gaskell, Elizabeth, *The Life Of Charlotte Brontë*, p. 108
17. Brontë, Charlotte, *Jane Eyre*, p. 65

Chapter 10

1. Gaskell, Elizabeth, *The Life Of Charlotte Brontë*, p. 199
2. Kambani, Marianna [Ed.], *The Lives of Victorian Literary Figures: the Brownings, the Brontës and the Rossettis by Their Contemporaries*, p. 147
3. Letter from Charlotte Brontë to Ellen Nussey, 21 March 1841, ms. Brontë Parsonage Museum, Haworth
4. Orel, Harold [Ed.], *The Brontës: Interviews And Recollections*, p. 29
5. Diary paper of Emily and Anne Brontë, 24 November 1834, ms. Brontë Parsonage Museum, Haworth
6. Barker, Juliet, *The Brontës*, p. 318
7. Gerin, Winifred, *Anne Brontë*, p. 23
8. Orel, Harold [Ed.], *The Brontës: Interviews And Recollections*, p. 25
9. Bottrell, William, *Traditions and Hearthside Stories of West Cornwall*, pp. 169-70
10. Brontë, Charlotte, *Villette*, p. 373

11. du Maurier, Daphne, *Vanishing Cornwall*, p. 160
12. Newbold, Margaret, *'The Branwell Saga', Brontë Studies 2002, Volume 27, Issue 1*, p. 24
13. Brontë, Emily, *Wuthering Heights*, p. 320
14. Letter from Charlotte Brontë to Ellen Nussey, 4 July 1834, ms. Huntington Library, California
15. Brontë, Anne, *The Tenant of Wildfell Hall*, p. 5
16. Letter from Charlotte Brontë to Branwell Brontë, 17 May 1832, ms. Brontë Parsonage Museum, Haworth

Chapter 11

1. From *Reminiscences of Charlotte Brontë by Ellen Nussey, Scribner's Magazine*, May 1871
2. Ibid.
3. Letter from Charlotte Brontë to Ellen Nussey, 13 December 1846, ms. Huntington Library, California
4. Barnard, Louise and Barnard, Robert, *A Brontë Encyclopedia*, p. 108
5. Alexander, Christine [Ed.], *Tales of Glass Town, Angria, and Gondal*, p. 3
6. This teapot is now at the Brontë Parsonage Museum, Haworth
7. Hardy, Robert Spence, *William Grimshaw, Incumbent of Haworth*, p. 42
8. Southey, Robert, *The Life of Wesley, and the Rise and Progress of Methodism*, p. 188
9. Orel, Harold [Ed.], *The Brontës: Interviews And Recollections*, p. 25
10. As confirmed by handwriting expert Jean Elliott, MBIGdip
11. Brontë Manuscript Notebook, Brotherton Library, Leeds
12. Ibid.
13. Brontë, Anne, *The Tenant of Wildfell Hall*, p. 138
14. Letter from Patrick Brontë to Elizabeth Franks, 6 July 1835, ms. Brontë Parsonage Museum, Haworth
15. Ibid.
16. Letter from Ellen Nussey to Elizabeth Gaskell, 15 November 1855, ms. Brotherton Library, Leeds
17. Letter from James la Trobe to William Scruton, ms. Brontë Parsonage Museum, Haworth
18. Watson, Richard, *The Life of the Rev. John Wesley, A.M.*, pp. 51-2
19. Gerin, Winifred, *Anne Brontë*, p. 121

Chapter 12

1. Gaskell, Elizabeth, *The Life Of Charlotte Brontë*, p. 198-9
2. Diary paper of Emily and Anne Brontë, 24 November 1834, ms. Brontë Parsonage Museum, Haworth
3. Letter from Ellen Nussey to Elizabeth Gaskell, 15 November 1857, ms. Brotherton Library, Leeds
4. Matus, Jill L. [Ed.], *The Cambridge Companion to Elizabeth Gaskell*, p. 18
5. Green, Dudley [Ed.], *The Letters Of The Reverend Patrick Brontë*, p. 258

6. Gaskell, Elizabeth, *The Life Of Charlotte Brontë*, p. 199
7. Orel, Harold [Ed.], *The Brontës: Interviews And Recollections*, p. 25
8. Letter from Ellen Nussey to Elizabeth Gaskell, 15 November 1857, ms. Brotherton Library, Leeds
9. Edgerley, C. Mabel, '*Elizabeth Branwell – The "Small, Antiquated Lady"'*, *Brontë Society Transactions 1937, Volume 9, Issue 2*, p. 111
10. Letter from Branwell Brontë to Francis Grundy, 25 October 1842; Smith, Margaret (Ed.), *The Letters of Charlotte Brontë,* Volume 1, p. 294
11. Gaskell, Elizabeth, *The Life Of Charlotte Brontë,* p. 94
12. This piano, now restored, can be seen in the Brontë Parsonage Museum, Haworth
13. *Bradford Observer*, 10 April 1834
14. Lister, Philip, *Ghosts & Gravestones of Haworth*, p. 12
15. Letter from Branwell Brontë to Secretary, Royal Academy of Arts, 1835, ms. Brontë Parsonage Museum, Haworth
16. Du Maurier, Daphne, *The Infernal World of Branwell Brontë*, p. 47
17. Barker, Juliet, *The Brontës,* p. 227

Chapter 13

1. Letter from Charlotte Brontë to Rev. Henry Nussey, 9 May 1841, ms. William Self collection
2. Diary paper of Anne Brontë, 30 July 1841, ms. Law collection
3. These cards are referred to in Charlotte Brontë's letter to Ellen Nussey, 17 March 1840
4. The monument to William Weightman, paid for by the parishioners, is the largest in St Michael and All Angels' church.
5. Letter from Charlotte Brontë to Ellen Nussey, 20 January 1842, ms. Brontë Parsonage Museum, Haworth
6. Barker, Juliet, *The Brontës*, pp. 374-5
7. Charlotte Brontë's Roe Head Journal, ms. Brontë Parsonage Museum, Haworth
8. Diary paper of Emily Brontë, 31 July 1841, ms. Law collection
9. Letter from Charlotte Brontë to Ellen Nussey, 19 July 1841, ms. Brontë Parsonage Museum, Haworth
10. Barker, Juliet, *The Brontës*, pp. 361
11. Letter from Charlotte Brontë to Elizabeth Branwell, 29 September 1841
12. Ibid.
13. MacEwan, Helen, *The Brontës in Brussels*, p. 19
14. Letter from Branwell Brontë to Francis Grundy, 25 October 1842

Chapter 14

1. The 1850 General Board of Health inspection undertaken by Benjamin Herschel Babbage, showed, for example, an average age at death of 19.6 years in 1838.
2. Letter from Anne Brontë to Ellen Nussey, 26 January 1848, ms. Brontë Parsonage Museum, Haworth
3. du Maurie, Daphne, *The Infernal World of Branwell Brontë*, p. 156

4. Letter from Branwell Brontë to Francis Grundy, 29 October 1842
5. Barker, Juliet, *The Brontës*, p. 404
6. Last will and testament of Elizabeth Branwell, 30 April 1833, ms. National Archives, London
7. Ibid
8. Ibid.
9. Letter from Charlotte Brontë to Emily Brontë, 19 December 1843
10. Orel, Harold, *The Brontes: Interviews And Recollections*, pp. 61-62
11. Brontë, Charlotte, *Biographical Notice of Ellis and Acton Bell*, ms. British Library, London
12. Ibid.
13. Hargreaves, G.D., *'The Publishing of Poems by Currer, Ellis and Acton Bell'*, *Brontë Society Transactions 1969*, Volume 15, Issue 4, p. 294

Chapter 15

1. Hargreaves, G.D., *'The Publishing of "Poems by Currer, Ellis and Acton Bell"'*, *Brontë Society Transactions 1969*, Volume 15, Issue 4, p. 295
2. *Athenaem*, 4 July 1846
3. The autographs of Currer, Ellis and Acton Bell sent to Mr. Enoch are at the Brontë Parsonage Museum, Haworth
4. Letter from Charlotte Brontë to Thomas de Quincey, 16 June 1847
5. Hargreaves, G.D., *'The Publishing of "Poems by Currer, Ellis and Acton Bell"'*, *Brontë Society Transactions 1969*, Volume 15, Issue 4, p. 298
6. Brontë, Charlotte, *Jane Eyre*, pp. 337-8
7. Brontë, Anne, *The Tenant of Wildfell Hall*, p. 104
8. Brontë Manuscript Notebook, Brotherton Library, Leeds
9. *The Rambler*, September 1848
10. Letter from Charlotte Brontë to W.S. Williams, 5 September 1850, ms. Princeton University, New Jersey
11. Smith, George, *George Smith: a Memoir, With Some Pages of Autobiography*, p. 89
12. The original Bradshaw's timetable for this journey can be seen at the Search Engine Archives, National Railway Museum, York
13. *'A Portrait of Lydia Robinson'*, *Brontë Studies 1981*, Volume 18, Issue 1, p. 29
14. Letter from Charlotte Brontë to Ellen Nussey, 23 November 1848, ms. Brontë Parsonage Museum, Haworth
15. Brontë, Anne, *Agnes Grey*, p. 144
16. Rhodes, Philip, *'A Medical Appraisal Of The Brontës'*, *Brontë Society Transactions 1972*, Volume 16, Issue 2, p. 106

Chapter 16

1. Letter from Charlotte Brontë to W.S. Williams, 22 May 1850, ms. Princeton University, New Jersey
2. Nussey, Ellen, *A Short Account Of The Last Days Of Dear A.B.*, ms. King's School Library, Canterbury

3. Gaskell, Elizabeth, *The Life Of Charlotte Brontë*, p. 379
4. Brontë, Charlotte, *Shirley*, pp. 461-2
5. Brontë, Charlotte, *Shirley*, p. 463
6. Barker, Juliet, *The Brontës*, p. 685
7. Letter from Charlotte Brontë to Margaret Wooler, 22 September 1851
8. Letter from Charlotte Brontë to Ellen Nussey, 14 August 1840, ms. Brontë Parsonage Museum, Haworth
9. Hardie-Budden, Melissa, '*Maternal Forebears of the Brontë Archive: 'Nothing Comes from Nothing'; or Stories from Another Canon*', *Brontë Studies 2015, Volume 40, Issue 4*, p. 270
10. Gerin, Winifred, *Emily Brontë*, p. 259
11. Letter from Charlotte Brontë to Ellen Nussey, 27 May 1853, ms. Brontë Parsonage Museum, Haworth
12. Rowe, J. Hambley, '*The Maternal Relatives of the Brontës*', *Brontë Society Transactions 1923, Volume 6, Issue 33*, p. 135
13. *Yorkshire Evening Post*, 20 May 1942

Chapter 17

1. Kingston, Rev. John, '*Memoirs of the Life of John Kingston, Preacher of the Gospel*', *The Methodist Magazine for the Year 1799, Volume XXII*, p. 209
2. Kingston, Rev. John, '*Memoirs of the Life of John Kingston, Preacher of the Gospel*', *The Methodist Magazine for the Year 1799, Volume XXII*, p. 365
3. *Journal of the Conference*, 1807
4. Letter from Eliza Kingston to her nephew Joseph Kingston Burgster
5. Ratchford, Fannie E., '*The Loneliness of a Brontë Cousin*', *Brontë Society Transactions 1957, Volume 13, Issue 2*, p. 102
6. Kingston, John, *The New Pocket Biographical Dictionary, Second Edition*, p. iv
7. Kingston, John, *The New Pocket Biographical Dictionary, Second Edition*, p. 299
8. Kingston, John, *The New Pocket Biographical Dictionary, Second Edition*, p. 306
9. Newbold, Margaret, '*The Branwell Saga*', *Brontë Studies 2002, Volume 27, Issue 1*, p. 20
10. Ratchford, Fannie E., '*The Loneliness of a Brontë Cousin*', *Brontë Society Transactions 1957, Volume 13, Issue 2*, p. 102
11. Last will and testament of Elizabeth Branwell, 30 April 1833, ms. National Archives, London
12. Ratchford, Fannie E., '*The Loneliness of a Brontë Cousin*', *Brontë Society Transactions 1957, Volume 13, Issue 2*, p. 103
13. Ratchford, Fannie E., '*The Loneliness of a Brontë Cousin*', *Brontë Society Transactions 1957, Volume 13, Issue 2*, p. 107
14. Ibid.
15. Ibid.
16. Details from the 1871 census of Penzance.
17. Ratchford, Fannie E., '*The Loneliness of a Brontë Cousin*', *Brontë Society Transactions 1957, Volume 13, Issue 2*, p. 109-10

18. Ratchford, Fannie E., *'The Loneliness of a Brontë Cousin'*, *Brontë Society Transactions 1957, Volume 13, Issue 2*, p. 109
19. Rowe, J. Hambley, *'The Maternal Relatives of the Brontës'*, *Brontë Society Transactions 1923, Volume 6, Issue 33*, p. 144
20. Rowe, J. Hambley, *'The Maternal Relatives of the Brontës'*, *Brontë Society Transactions 1923, Volume 6, Issue 33*, p. 143-4

Chapter 18

1. Letter from Charlotte Brontë to Ellen Nussey, 4 January 1838, ms. Brontë Parsonage Museum, Haworth
2. Gaskell, Elizabeth, *The Life of Charlotte Brontë*, pp. 96-7
3. Chadwick, Ellis H., *In the Footsteps of the Brontës*, p. 185
4. Letter from Charlotte Brontë to Ellen Nussey, 1 July 1841
5. Gaskell, Elizabeth, *The Life Of Charlotte Brontë*, pp. 180-181

Select Bibliography

ALEXANDER, Christine and **SELLARS**, Jane, *The Art of the Brontës*, Cambridge University Press, 1995

ALEXANDER, Christine (Ed.), *Tales of Glass Town, Angria, and Gondal (Introduction)*, Oxford World's Classics, 2010

BARKER, Juliet, *The Brontës*, Weidenfeld & Nicolson, 1994

BARNARD, Robert and Louise (Ed.), *A Brontë Encyclopedia*, Blackwell, 2007

BOTTRELL, William, *Traditions and Hearthside Stories of West Cornwall*, W. Cornish, 1873

CARTER, Clive, *The Port of Penzance: A History*, Black Dwarf, 1998

CHADWICK, Ellis H., *In the Footsteps of the Brontës*, Pitman, 1913

CHITHAM, Edward, *A Life of Emily Brontë*, Blackwell, 1987

DINSDALE, Ann, *The Brontës At Haworth*, Frances Lincoln, 2006

DU MAURIER, Daphne, *The Infernal World of Branwell Brontë*, Penguin, 1972

DU MAURIER, Daphne, *Vanishing Cornwall*, Penguin, 1972

GASKELL, Elizabeth, *The Life of Charlotte Brontë*, Penguin Classics, 1985

GÉRIN, Winifred, *Anne Brontë*, Allen Lane, 1959

GREEN, Dudley, *Patrick Brontë Father of Genius*, The History Press, 2008

GREEN, Dudley, [Ed.], *The Letters Of The Reverend Patrick Brontë*, Nonsuch, 2005

HARDIE-BUDDEN, Melissa, *Penzance 2000*, Penzance Town Council, 2000

GRUNDY, Francis, *Pictures of The Past*, Griffith & Farrar, 1879

HOLLAND, Nick, *In Search of Anne Brontë*, The History Press, 2016

HOLLAND, Nick, *Emily Brontë: A Life in Twenty Poems*, The History Press, 2018

INGHAM, Patricia, *The Brontës*, Oxford University Press, 2008

LEMON, Charles, *Classics Of Brontë Scholarship*, The Bronte Society, 1999

LEYLAND, Francis, *The Brontë Family*, Hurst & Blackett, 1886

LISTER, Philip, *Ghosts & Gravestones of Haworth*, Tempus, 2006

LONOFF, Sue, *The Belgian Essays: A Critical Edition*, Yale University Press, 1997

MACEWAN, Helen, *The Brontës in Brussels*, Peter Owen, 2014

NEUFELDT, Victor A. (Ed.), *The Works Of Patrick Branwell Brontë: 1837-1848*, Psychology Press, 1997

OREL, Harold, *The Brontës: Interviews And Recollections*, Palgrave MacMillan, 1996

SAGAR-FENTON, Mike, *Penzance: The Biography,* Amberley Publishing, 2015

SHORTER, Clement, *The Brontës and Their Circle*, J.M. Dent, 1914

SHORTER, Clement, *The Brontës' Life and Letters*, Cambridge University Press, 2013

SMITH, Margaret (ed.), *The Letters Of Charlotte Brontë (Volumes 1-3)*, Clarendon Press, 1995

SELECT BIBLIOGRAPHY

SOUTHEY, Robert, *The Life of Wesley, and the Rise and Progress of Methodism*, Longman, 1820

SPARK, Muriel, *The Essence of The Brontës*, Peter Owen, 1993

SUGDEN, K.A.R., *A Short History of the Brontës*, Oxford University Press, 1929

The versions of books by the Brontë sisters referred to in the notes and text are as follows:

Bell, C., E., and A., Poems by Currer, Ellis, And Acton Bell, Aylott & Jones, 1846

Brontë, Anne, Agnes Grey, Wordsworth Classics, 1998

Brontë, Anne, The Tenant Of Wildfell Hall, Wordsworth Classics, 1994

Brontë, Charlotte, Jane Eyre, Wordsworth Classics, 1999

Brontë, Charlotte, Shirley, Collins Classics, 2012

Brontë, Charlotte, The Professor, Wordsworth Classics, 2010

Brontë, Emily, Wuthering Heights, Penguin Classics, 1985

Index

INDEX